FOUR INDISPENSABLE GUIDES®
TO NORTHERN NEW MEXICO

Compiled and published by a joint venture of
INSIDE SANTA FE AND TAOS, Inc.
(publishers of a monthly journal for visitors)
and
CERRO GORDO PUBLISHING CO., Inc

The section on Santa Fe is based on an article by John Ehrlichman which first appeared in *Travel & Leisure* magazine and has been recently revised.

Printed
in
New Mexico,
U.S.A.

ISBN 0-9618101-1-4

INDEX

For Suzanne and Gary,
with the hope that you
will use this and come
see us one of these days.

John Ehrlichman
12.29.89

SANTA FE

by John Ehrlichman

In the years I've lived in Santa Fe, our little town has endured some of the vicissitudes of media attention experienced by young debutantes and just-launched actresses. A decade and a half ago, alas, Santa Fe was discovered. Never mind that it had been here since 1610, and had been a Territorial capital under the Spanish, Mexicans and Americans. In the mid-Seventies, Esquire and Women's Wear Daily splashed news of Santa Fe all over their pages. With its pop debut, the old town saw an unreal real estate boom and an influx of trendy folk who preempted all the tables in the good restaurants, ran up the price of turquoise jewelry and made it impossible to find a place to park downtown "in season."

The good news is that the debutante has been jilted by all those good-time Charlies. I guess they have decided to hold hands with Positano and Xi'an these days. The feverish blush is off the maiden's lovely cheek, and she's settled down. She's as attractive as she ever was, but she's gotten over some of her fancy airs.

We're inviting our friends to come visit Santa Fe again, with some confidence that they'll be pleased with what they find. This year the Santa Fe Opera has scheduled a repertoire that ordinary folks will enjoy. There's a real chance that this summer hotel prices will come down some, according to Michael Cerletti, one of our leading hoteliers. And the enduring qualities of this place are as singular and wonderful as they ever were. The sun still shines through air that is exhilarating. We're on a bench of piñon-dotted land at 7,000 feet, backed by the Sangre de Cristo Mountains which rise to 12,000 feet just northeast of the town.

The light—especially at sunrise and sunset—must be experienced. When we have visitors come to town, we encourage them to spend some quiet time on our flat roof, where at dusk they can see the mountains and the foothills washed by the changing sunlight. We want our friends to be able to carry away the extraordinary sense of uplift we feel in this place just then.

Some of our visitors have assumed that Santa Fe is a dusty frontier village out on the desert flats. They've arrived without coats, rain gear and the other essentials of Rocky Mountain life, so our hall closet is full of extra ponchos and wide-brimmed hats kept just for them. It rains here in the summertime; in August you can usually set your clock by the afternoon deluge. When it isn't raining, the humidity is blessedly low, between 15 and 25 percent most of the time.

The town has grown some in 15 years, but it has managed to maintain a humane, civilized scale that harmonizes with its glorious setting. Partly by planning, mostly by chance, franchise food places and much of the other architectural schlock have been gathered on one street south of the main part of town. There are a few five-story buildings near the Plaza now, and they seem to me unduly massive, but the requisite adobe color helps to shrink them.

Three of these big buildings are downtown hotels, and they are part of the good news for travelers. There was a time when the choice of accommodations

New Mexico's

State Bird

The Chaparral Bird, commonly known as the Roadrunner, is a member of the cuckoo family. The Roadrunner has a bill nearly half its body length and a tufted head. Although it is usually seen running along the ground, it can fly at low levels. Beep beep.

was quite limited, but now visitors find condominium rentals, good motels with pools and playgrounds, and hotels providing everything from modest $49 *casitas* to luxurious suites with a view, as in the Eldorado Hotel. At the best times—during Indian Market in August, Fiesta de Santa Fe in September, and throughout the ski season—there are usually plenty of rooms to choose from in all categories, if you make reservations in advance.

I think Santa Fe once was a difficult place to explore well, but that situation is also improving. We like to take our friends to off-the-beaten-track restaurants like Tomasita's and Tecolote Cafe where the food is the local fare, reliably wonderful (and inexpensive). Some of the best things to see and do are outside of town, in the little old Spanish villages tucked into mountain valleys, and at the pueblos, the Indian communities up and down the Rio Grande Valley. It's easier nowadays to find out about such things, since local tour companies provide assistance in making reservations and arranging tours and private guides.

We usually persuade our friends to begin their visit at the Palace of the Governors, which for nearly 300 years served as the seat of government. The museum in the Palace has been organized to explain the history of Santa Fe and the region, and some exhibits show how the building itself was constructed and used. Across the courtyard of the museum, there are exhibits of traditional Indian culture (which seems entirely proper, since rebellious Pueblo Indians re-captured Santa Fe from the Spanish and used the palace as a kiva for about a dozen years in the late 17th century). We recommend the museum's store as one of the most reliable shops in the center of town for contemporary Indian crafts. And under the portal of the palace, artisans from the nearby pueblos sell jewelry, pottery, weavings and big round loaves of bread that have been baked in the beehive-shaped adobe *hornos* behind their homes.

Nearby is the Plaza, a square of trees and benches and open space that has always been the center of Santa Fe's community life. On the Fourth of July, local service clubs hold a big pancake breakfast in the Plaza for everyone. All through the summer, there are entertainments and craft fairs here. When the Olympic torch-bearers ran through Santa Fe, crowds gathered at the Plaza to watch the governor and mayor greet them.

At Christmas—a magic time in Santa Fe—the old territorial adobe buildings surrounding the Plaza are topped with rows of the traditional *farolitos*—candles in brown paper bags. On an evening near Christmas Eve, a version of the age-old Spanish ceremony of Las Posadas is enacted. Joseph leads Mary on a donkey from inn to inn seeking shelter. They are followed by a group singing the customary old Spanish songs at each stop. Joseph and Mary are turned away from every door by the devil in a shiny red suit with a long, forked tail. At last, they are taken in at one inn's manger amid joyous song. Then cookies and hot cocoa are served around a bonfire.

The Plaza is also the setting for the fabulous Indian Market, held the third weekend in August. Hundreds of skilled Native American artists and artisans submit their best work to a panel of judges. The top 450 are permitted to sell their weavings, pots, jewelry, kachinas, wood carvings and other crafts in booths that fill the Plaza. Collectors come from everywhere to bargain and buy, the galleries in town put on special shows, and it's a big social weekend, too. If you'd like to see it, make your room and restaurant reservations early; some regulars book a year ahead.

Some of the big-money collectors and dealers begin to gather in the Indian Market at about 5 a.m. on Saturday, especially around the booths of the best-known Indian artists, potters and jewelers displaying their prize-winning entries. We like to arrive about 6 a.m. to see what happens when the most popular exhibitors show up and feverish buying begins. Around the edge of the Plaza, there is plenty of coffee and Indian fry bread with honey for sale in the early hours.

In late July, there is also the Spanish Market, during which Hispanic artisans gather in the Plaza to sell their traditional crafts—wood carving, tinwork, ironwork, painting and weaving. And any time of year you'll find a number of reliable shops set around the Plaza. Among them, Packard's, Dewey's Gallery and James Reid's are worthwhile places to browse among the arts and crafts. Just off the southeast corner of the Plaza is La Fonda Hotel, the historic old inn at the end of the Santa Fe Trail. Modernized now, it has welcomed travelers with food, drink and a bed since the days of the covered wagon. The lobby of La Fonda is a lively place, and its rooftop bar serves up broad vistas and cool drinks at sunset.

For a town of its size, Santa Fe provides a remarkably rich and diverse menu of music, theater and art. On a summer evening, you can dine at a restaurant where a guitarist or ensemble provides subtle background music. After dinner, your choices range from grand opera to hard rock.

In July and August, the world-famous Santa Fe Opera mounts its elaborate productions in a mostly covered, open-sided opera house in Tesuque, just a little north of town. When the repertoire is popular, tickets can be scarce. You should order tickets ahead (telephone 505/982-3855) and ask for seats under cover; about 10 rows are open to the weather. Performances begin at 9 p.m., and remember to take a blanket and jacket, since around midnight even the warmest summer evening turns chilly.

Held at about the same time, the Santa Fe Chamber Music Festival attracts internationally renowned artists and composers for a variety of performances and symposia in a near-perfect setting, the St. Francis Auditorium on Palace Avenue (983-2075 for schedules and information). At intermission, you can buy libations—and ice cream cones.

Add to these major attractions the year-round performances by two orchestras and a chorale, several concert series, three active dramatic theaters and occasional visits by touring dance companies. Downtown you will find a jazz club, a couple of dine-and-dance places, and several bars where pianists play real loud. In summer, we always take visitors to the Sheraton Hotel to see the Maria Benitez Dance Company, a large and talented troupe that performs *flamenco* as it should be done (982-5591 for information).

These are just some of the markets and special events that fill Santa Fe's calendar—especially in summer. Once you've seen the Plaza and perhaps surveyed the town on one of the scheduled tours, you'll want to backtrack and do some leisurely exploring. We make a point of taking friends to the Museum of International Folk Art and the Wheelwright Museum of the American Indian, set next to each other on Camino Lejo. If my wife and I traveled to your hometown, I would probably be reluctant to visit your museums; so you can be certain that if these two weren't truly remarkable I wouldn't send you up the hill to see them. The first has a huge and beautifully displayed collection of folk art from around the world, decorated and mounted by the architect and designer Alexander Girard. The second is filled with the fine art of Native Americans and has a first-rate trading post downstairs.

Canyon Road is the old wood-gatherers' trail, and along a six-block section of it you'll find dozens of galleries and shops, craftsmen at work, and several good restaurants. If your Canyon Road time is limited, at least be sure to stop at these places:

The Linda Durham Gallery (400 Canyon Road), in an old schoolhouse at the corner of Garcia Street, displays quality contemporary painting, sculpture and constructions. Bellas Artes, Ltd., just behind Linda Durham's, sells wonderful pre-Columbian and textile art and crafts. Morning Star Gallery (513 Canyon Road) is for Indian artifacts—and it's one of my wife's favorites. Robert F. Nichols (No. 419) is filled with antiques and folk art, Native American art, great quilts and other Americana. Munson Gallery (No. 225) is an excellent gallery of painting and sculpture. Volker de la Harpe (No. 707) features woodwork, especially carved doors. At Glassworks (No. 821), a glassblower plies his craft. The Shop of the Frightened Owl (No. 1117) has unusual art, antiques and old jewelry.

If you get hungry en route have lunch at El Farol (No. 808; 983-9912). The *tapas* are delicious. This is a place to have dinner, too. We always guide folks to two special galleries near Canyon Road. One is the Fenn Gallery (1075 Paseo de Peralta), which displays art ranging from the works of great masters to Doug Hyde's excellent contemporary Indian sculpture. Ask to see the guesthouse and gardens; the personal collection of Indian art is extraordinary. And the second place is the Gerald Peters Gallery in a fine old home at 439 Camino del Monte Sol. It concentrates on art with a Southwest flavor, which includes works by Charles Russell and artists of the Taos School as well as contemporary pieces of top quality.

Back in the center of town, the Elaine Horwitch Gallery (129 W. Palace Ave.) features lively contemporary art full of Indians, cowboys, coyotes and Southwestern landscapes. Look here, too, for the work of David Hockney and Fritz Scholder and for some quality jewelry. Santa Fe East (200 Old Santa Fe Trail) is in a handsome adobe and sells a wide range of painting, sculpture and designer jewelry.

Davis Mather Folk Art Gallery (141 Lincoln Ave.) is a tiny space full of remarkable carved wooden animals, watermelons and wedding figures, tin-work and folk painting. We like the big pigs. And Dewey Galleries (74 E. San Francisco St., on the Plaza) shows quality American Western art—always worth seeing—plus outstanding baskets, jewelry and other Indian work.

The Chamber of Commerce says there are more than 125 art galleries in Santa Fe. No one I know has seen all of them. My list doubtlessly leaves out some great ones that I've just never prowled. Half the fun of the town is browsing and discovering wonderful things on your own. For example, there is a little shop called the Holbrook Gallery (402 Old Santa Fe Trail), which shows Asian, African and American antique art and artifacts, well described and reasonably priced. I never fail to admire what I see there. Like the Frightened Owl on Canyon Road, Holbrook's is one of those places that are too easy to overlook if you're not a determined explorer.

And some of the good art in Santa Fe isn't in any gallery. Artists like painter Forrest Moses (982-4160) and potter Rick Dillingham (983-3447) work in their homes, and sometimes they will show their artwork by special arrangement. Dillingham is also a consultant to institutions and other major buyers of Southwestern art.

The city of Santa Fe is a focal point of an intriguing mountain region that begins just north of Albuquerque and extends 150 miles north to Taos. You can get to know this area on several easy one-day trips. I don't think any visit to Santa Fe should fail to include a drive on the High Road to Taos or to nearby cliff dwellings and Spanish villages. Here are some of our favorite short trips out of town:

If you're in Santa Fe the first Sunday of June, July, August or September, drive six miles south on Interstate 25 to the La Cienega Exit, then follow the signs to El Rancho de Las Golondrinas and the privately endowed Old Cienega Village Museum. This 400-acre restoration includes a chapel, shops and a *torreon*, or fortress tower, and shows the complex world of an old Spanish hacienda—much the same way

New Mexico's

State Fossil

New Mexico is one of the few states to have an official fossil, the Coelophysis dinosaur, a species extinct since the close of the Triassic period (200,000,000 years ago). This active carnivor was small, hollow-boned, stood like a bird, had blade-sharp teeth and a long tail. A famous example of this extinct species was found near Ghost Ranch (near Abiquiu on NM Highway #84).

that Williamsburg depicts Atlantic Colonial life. A blacksmith forges in his shop, vintners work in the winery, herders tend the sheep and cattle. And during the spring festival the first Sunday in May and the harvest festival the first Sunday in October, you can see traditional dancing, *conquistadores* on horseback, browse in an old-fashioned market and sample various colonial foods. It takes the better part of a day (the ranch is open 10 a.m. to 6 p.m.) to see this living museum well. Telephone 471-2261 for information.

The Pecos National Monument is about 45 minutes east of Santa Fe on Interstate 25 (take the exit to Pecos, then at the T intersection in Pecos, turn right and drive about four miles). Here are the ruins of a huge Spanish Colonial mission, and excavations revealing a large 12th century pueblo. Greer Garson and her late husband (whose ranch adjoins the monument) donated a truly excellent visitor's center containing artifacts and descriptions of the pueblo and offering a good film of the history of the area narrated by Miss Garson. Call 988-6340 for information.

About an hour's drive northwest of Santa Fe, Bandelier National Monument is a big hit with our guests and especially with their children. This 46-square-mile reserve has a good interpretive center (be sure to see the slide show), and there are all kinds of self-guided hikes—both short and long—to Anasazi ruins and cave dwellings that the kids and limber adults are allowed to enter. This site of ancient civilization is very close to the Los Alamos nuclear and laser facilities, and the implications of this juxtaposition are not lost on most visitors.

Another ancient civilization can be seen at the Puye Cliff Dwellings on the Santa Clara Pueblo's lands. Heading west on Route 4, you turn north about a mile after crossing the Rio Grande. Then drive six miles, and watch for signs. Once you've visited the ruins and enjoyed the beautiful views, you might want to continue up the canyon for a picnic in Santa Clara Pueblo's well maintained forests. There is a small fee for fishing in the stocked lakes or stream.

I feel a bit sorry for the folks who try to see Santa Fe in one day, stopping over while driving from Uncle Arnold's in Phoenix to Aunt Tillie's in Dallas.

This is a region of profoundly interesting history encompassing geology, archaeology and the ebb and flow of ancient peoples. The texture and form of the geography have been brilliantly depicted by the late Georgia O'Keeffe, who lived in Abiquiu, northwest of Santa Fe. Such landscapes demand that you take time to sit and really see them. There is a wonderful diversity of people to get acquainted with, some great food to be sampled and countless galleries and shops to explore. In my opinion, to do it right requires five or six days, at least.

The best time of year in the region is the autumn. The aspens turn the Sangre de Cristos a bright gold, and the cottonwoods along the streambeds explode into rich yellows, then golds and finally browns before their leaves are blown away. October weather is usually bright, sunny and clear, with crisp nights full of stars. By then, the restaurants and roads are not overloaded with travelers. I like to walk around town in the fall; Santa Fe is just the right size for rambling. There's time for poking into the galleries to see what they are showing, for running into people you know and, perhaps, for sitting awhile on a bench in the sunshine to watch what's going on in the Plaza.

I recommend it.

Downtown Santa Fe

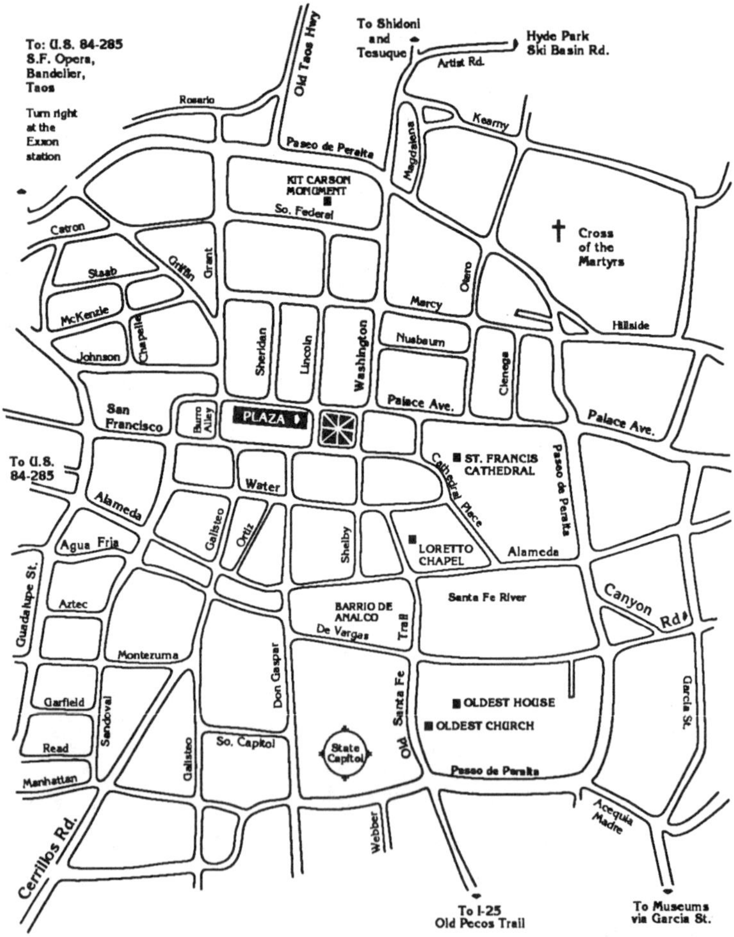

To: U.S. 84-285
S.F. Opera,
Bandelier,
Taos

Turn right at the Exxon station

Old Taos Hwy

To Shidoni and Tesuque

Hyde Park Ski Basin Rd.

Artist Rd.

Rosario

Kearny

Paseo de Peralta

Magdalena

KIT CARSON MONUMENT

So. Federal

Catron

Cross of the Martyrs

Staab

Griffin

Grant

Otero

McKenzie

Mercy

Hillside

Chapelle

Johnson

Sheridan

Lincoln

Washington

Nusbaum

Cienega

San Francisco

Burro Alley

PLAZA

Palace Ave.

Palace Ave.

To U.S. 84-285

ST. FRANCIS CATHEDRAL

Cathedral Place

Paseo de Peralta

Water

Alameda

Galisteo

Ortiz

Shelby

LORETTO CHAPEL

Alameda

Agua Fria

Guadalupe St.

Aztec

Santa Fe River

Canyon Rd.

BARRIO DE ANALCO

De Vargas

Trail

Montezuma

Don Gaspar

Old Santa Fe

Garfield

Sandoval

OLDEST HOUSE

OLDEST CHURCH

Garcia St.

Read

Galisteo

So. Capitol

State Capitol

Manhattan

Paseo de Peralta

Acequia Madre

Cerrillos Rd.

Webber

To I-25 Old Pecos Trail

To Museums via Garcia St.

VISITING SANTA FE

GETTING THERE Santa Fe is 63 miles northeast of Albuquerque's airport, which is served by most major airlines. The best plan is to rent a car for the drive, or reserve a seat on the Shuttlejack (982-4311), the direct bus service from the Albuquerque Airport to several Santa Fe hotels. Local cabs can take you from a Shuttlejack destination to your chosen motel, condo or hotel.

INFORMATION AND GUIDANCE The helpful staff at the *Santa Fe Convention and Visitors Bureau* (201 West Marcy St., Santa Fe, NM 87501; telephone 505/984-6760) can supply the dates for markets and special events, answer questions, and provide lists of restaurants, brochures and maps.

There are also several local companies ready and willing to help make arrangements for your visit. For example, *Discover Santa Fe, Inc.* (924 Paseo de Peralta; 982-4979) will make hotel reservations and set up guided jaunts around town or out into the country on all-day trips ($25 an hour). Many of its guides also work at Santa Fe's outstanding museums and can help visitors buy local jewelry, pottery or weaving of good quality. Other services, among them *Santa Fe Detours* (La Fonda Hotel; 800/338-6877; 983-6565) reserve rooms, guides and tours, too.

When you arrive, if you haven't booked one of the guide services, you might want to get oriented by signing up for one of the in-season tours (June-August), which are really worthwhile. *Waite Thompson's Walking Tours* takes you to and explains the principal historic attractions in about 2-1/2 hours. Thompson also walks you through a residential area, talks some about the local architecture, and makes a stop for refreshments on Canyon Road. The tour begins at La Fonda Hotel, in the morning and afternoon, year-round; it costs $10. Telephone 988-3548 or 983-6565 for information and reservations.

The Roadrunner, a division of Gray Line, is a little open-air jitney that covers some of the same ground and also visits the Wheelwright Museum. But it would be my second choice, because it zooms by some interesting places that deserve a slower pace. The 1-1/2 hour tour begins at Palace and Lincoln Avenue four times a day; it costs $6. For information, telephone 983-9491.

WHERE TO STAY Of Santa Fe's 3,700 motel and hotel rooms, some are quite fancy. *The Clarion Eldorado Hotel* (309 W. San Francisco St.; 800/762-2333; 988-4455), has five floors and 218 rooms, a rooftop pool, three restaurants, a lounge, valet parking and convention facilities. Some deluxe rooms even have fireplaces. Deluxe doubles cost $140-$180. Another entry is the *Inn on the Alameda* (Paseo de Peralta and Alameda; 984-2121). This small hotel, in traditional Southwest design, is just three blocks from the Plaza and has 36 rooms furnished with oversize beds. Prices for two are $125; mini-suite $200; suite $220. And the *Hotel St. Francis* (210 Don Gaspar Ave.; 983-5700) offers 85 rooms, some of them adjoining. This is a complete renovation of an old hotel in the center of town, and it includes a lounge, a restaurant just off the lobby, and afternoon tea. Double rooms cost $75-$125.

Two resort hotels just outside of town are renowned for premier accommodations. *Rancho Encantado* (Route 22 in Tesuque; 982-3537) provides hotel service in detached *casitas* and has an excellent dining room; nearby there are also one- and two-bedroom condos. All are beautifully furnished with native crafts. Pleasures include tennis, a pool, horses and a full ranch program. Summer through fall, double rates are $200 in a *casita*, $230-$300 in a condo. The ranch is closed January 2-March 21.

At *Bishop's Lodge* (Bishop's Lodge Rd.; 983-6377), there are 62 rooms and suites, plus a dining room and such activities as swimming, tennis and horseback riding. From June through August, double rates are $184-300, including breakfast and dinner and a full-day program for children ages 4-12.

Some hotels in town are so popular that more than half their rooms are booked by returning guests during the summer. Among those that must be doing a lot of things right is *La Posada de Santa Fe* (330 E. Palace Ave.; 983-6351), on six acres of land near the Plaza. Here there are dozens of older adobe *casitas*, some with fireplaces. La Posada has its own restaurant, bar and pool. Standard double rates are $75-$160; a suite costs $140-$300; a few *casitas* have kitchens.

Two miles south of the Plaza is *El Rey Inn* (1862 Cerrillos Rd.; 982-1931), a family-run motel on 3-1/2 acres with a pool, large playground, hot tub, and unusually attractive rooms and suites. Rooms begin at $42 for a double; some have kitchenettes beginning at $53; two-bedroom suites with kitchen are available at $96. Make reservations early!

There are dozens of other choices among the hotels and motels of Santa Fe, including the *Hilton*, which has just been remodeled and is around the corner from the Eldorado. Double rooms cost $119-$169. There are also a *Sheraton*, three *Best Westerns* and many independents. An unusual Best Western is the *Inn at Loretto* (211 Old Santa Fe Trail; 800/528-1234 or 505/988-5531), built to resemble a classic adobe pueblo. It has 139 rooms and suites and is located downtown, about two blocks from the Plaza. Double rooms and sofa-suites cost $130-$140 in July and August; a suite is $300.

Condominiums right in town can be rented on a daily basis. At *Otra Vez en Santa Fe* (Galisteo and Water Sts.; 988-2244) there are 18 fully equipped units. In June, condos with one bedroom cost $100, and those with two bedrooms, $125; during July and August, prices rise to $125 and $150, except during the Indian Market, when they are $165 and $200. September through May, daily rates are $100 and $125, except holidays.

Fort Marcy Compound (320 Artist Rd.; 982-9480) is comprised of 100 one–, two- and three-bedroom condominium units, many with views and fireplaces. Double rates in summer start at $92; the rest of the year, $82-$112.

Guesthouses are another attractive possibility for visitors. One family we know has a delightful little guesthouse just big enough for two in a residential neighborhood about a mile from the Plaza: *Polly's Guest House* (410 Camino Don Miguel; 983-9481). It's an adobe *casita* with its own kitchen, a little garden patio and parking. Rates are $45 a night or $300 a week. And John Zinn offers *Manzano House* (near Canyon Rd; 983-2054), a fully furnished adobe that sleeps four or more—and has wine for you on your arrival. The rate is $110 per day, $750 per week for a real home away from home.

Bed-and-breakfast places are popping up in villages all around Santa Fe. You can spend the night in Galisteo, Los Alamos, Truchas, Española and Chimayo. For information, write to New Mexico's Bed and Breakfast Association, Box 55, Lincoln, NM 88338.

Among several B&Bs right in Santa Fe is the *Grant Corner Inn* (122 Grant Ave.; 983-6678), with 11 rooms, great food and an elegant Victorian atmosphere. Rates for two are $50-$100 a day. And there is *Preston House* (106 Faithway St,; 982-3465), which friends of ours liked a lot. It is a pretty Queen Anne house where guests are welcomed with fresh flowers and fruit by helpful folks. Doubles cost $55-$125 a day. The newest addition to the Santa Fe B&B scene is the *Territorial Inn* at 215 Washington Ave.; 989-7737 with 10 rooms, a hot tub, a formal rose garden and antique Victorian furnishings. $80-$120 a day.

WHERE TO EAT The local Yellow Pages lists 17 pages of restaurants, ranging from funky to fancy and from awful to superb. Here's a short list of places we've found admirable (not including hotel dining rooms or cafeterias—some of which are pretty good).

Begin the day at the *Tecolote Cafe* (1203 Cerrillos Rd.), where favorite choices are the breakfast burrito, hotcakes and freshly baked rolls. Reservations are not accepted, but the food is worth the wait. *Pasqual's* (121 Don Gaspar, downtown) also attracts long lines. Here omelets, fruit breads and cobblers are hits. And the *Grant Corner Inn* (122 Grant Ave.; 983-6678) usually provides two gourmet choices in the morning—plus fruit frappes and pastries—in a Victorian atmosphere. Reservations are required.

No trip to Santa Fe is complete without lunch at *The Shed* (113-1/2 E. Palace Ave.), which serves primarily local food, but the hot chile sauce has been toned down a little. Musts include a side order of posole—marinated spiced hominy. Even if you don't like grits, you should try a cup of this local dish. And do order the mocha cake—it's as rich as Rockefeller. The no-reservations policy results in long lines. The Shed is open only until 2:30 p.m.; no credit cards are accepted.

Josie's Casa de Comida (225 E. Marcy St.) is the place for authentic local food and superb desserts. This is one of the few restaurants in America that always has baked apples. That alone gives Josie's six stars, but the entrees are wonderful, too. Neither reservations nor credit cards are accepted; long lines of Santa Feans wait for tables at noon. Lunch is served until 4 p.m. No other meal is offered.

Julian's (221 Shelby St.988-2355) is located just 1 1/2 blocks from the Plaza, and features *regional Italian cuisine*. Dinner seven days a week, lunch Monday - Friday 11:30 -2pm. Do make reservations.

Now, we have a problem. There are two dozen restaurants that I can heartily recommend for dinner, but there just isn't space enough to tell you about them all. One place you might otherwise overlook is *Tomasita's Santa Fe Station* (500 S. Guadalupe St.), which is so inexpensive and informal and serves such delicious food that local people hate to tell outsiders about it. The daily specials are more than reliable. The *sopaipillas* (puffs of deep-fried bread dough, about four inches square) are outstanding. I like my *sopaipillas* stuffed, but they are also good plain—with honey. Reservations are not accepted; lines of secretive locals wait. The same family has opened *Diego's Restaurant y Cantina* (988-5101) in DeVargas Mall, also inexpensive, informal and good.

The Pink Adobe (406 Old Santa Fe Trail; 983-7712) has everything: atmosphere, alert service and top-quality food and drink. Try the Creole and New Mexican specialties. Our favorite houseguest says the Steak Dunigan is the best piece of meat in the nation—it's topped with green chile and mushrooms. Reservations are a must.

Don't be put off by the cute name of *Santacafe* (231 Washington Ave.; 984-1788). The nouvelle food is excellent, and the setting is comfortable. In the summer you can dine by candlelight outside, under the big trees. Reservations are needed. Highly recommended.

The Coyote Cafe, upstairs at 132 West Water St. (983-1615) opened in the Spring, 1987, and was an immediate hit. A well-known chef and restaurateur, Mark Miller, presents a constantly changing and beautifully prepared menu which combines our local foods with his sophisticated flair. The decor is upbeat, the service excellent. Not inexpensive; figure $150 for four with wine. Reservations essential, perhaps far ahead during the summer.

The Compound (653 Canyon Rd.; 982-4353) is special. It's the only place in town that requires a coat and tie (sometimes I try to cheat, and Victor always scolds me), and the only place in the state consistently given four stars by the Mobil Guide. The food is continental, served with a flair (white gloves, even), and the interior design by Alexander Girard is beautiful. Reservations are essential, and dinner costs about $100 for two.

Zia Diner (326 S. Guadalupe; 988-7008) where you can get meat loaf, tapioca pudding, fresh fish, "modern American" food, in a deco setting. Bar, patio, credit cards.

New Mexico's

State Vegetables

New Mexico has two official vegetables, the tasty and vitamin-rich chile (*capsicum annum*) and the staple pinto bean rich in protein. Both vegetables are found all year in most local food markets and are widely featured in the native cuisine. Chile, both the young and zesty green and the ripe but milder red pods, have been adapted for designs in business logos, decorative designs for kitchen items and seemingly endless tourist trinkets. Strings of red chile (*ristras*) and Christmas wreaths are widely used to decorate New Mexican houses.

Out at 2434 Cerrillos Road, in the College Plaza Shopping Center is the *Old Mexico Grill* where the excellent fare is more Mexican than New Mexican, and our favorites are the fajitas, served on hot griddles. No reservations. 473-0338.

At *La Tertulia Restaurant* (416 Agua Fria St.; 988-2769) you can sample local specialties served by the Ortiz family in six rooms of an old convento. Be sure to try the chalupas and the outstanding margaritas. Reservations are needed.

If you're going to be in town longer, here's a quick list of some other places that we like for dinner:

La Casa Sena (with great singing waiters in the bar), 125 E. Palace Ave; 988-9232

Comme Chez Vous, 116 W. San Francisco St.; 984-0004

E. K. Mas, 319 S. Guadalupe St., 989-7121

El Farol, 808 Canyon Rd.; 983-9912

El Nido, Tesuque; 988-4340

Furr's Cafeteria, 187 Paseo de Peralta; 988-4431; no credit cards

Guadalupe Cafe, 313 S. Guadalupe St.; 982-9762

La Traviata, 95 W. Marcy St.; 984-1091

Nectarine, 319 S. Guadalupe; 986-1137; gourmet

Palace Restaurant, 142 W. Palace Ave.; 982-9891

Pranzo Ristoranti, 540 Montezuma; 984-2645

Rosedale Southwest Seafood Shop, 907 W. Alameda; 989-7411

San Francisco Street Bar & Grill, 114 W. San Francisco; 982-2044

Shohko Cafe, 321 Johnson St.; 983-7288

Steaksmith, at El Gancho on Old Las Vegas Highway; 988-3333

Vanessie, 434 W. San Francisco St.; 982-9966; short, generous menu; music

And finally, here are some tasty tips that fit into no specific part of the day:

At *Woolworth's* on the Plaza, you can try a "Frito pie" (a bag of Fritos into which Texas chili is poured). You eat it with a plastic spoon while sitting on a bench watching people on the Plaza. You'll be taken for a local.

Stop by the *French Pastry Shop* in La Fonda Hotel for coffee and pastry, also baguettes, croissants and quiches.

The *Bobcat Bite*, 10 minutes out of town on the Old Las Vegas Highway, has the best hamburgers around—and the most hummingbirds.

Santa Fe Museums and Canyon Road

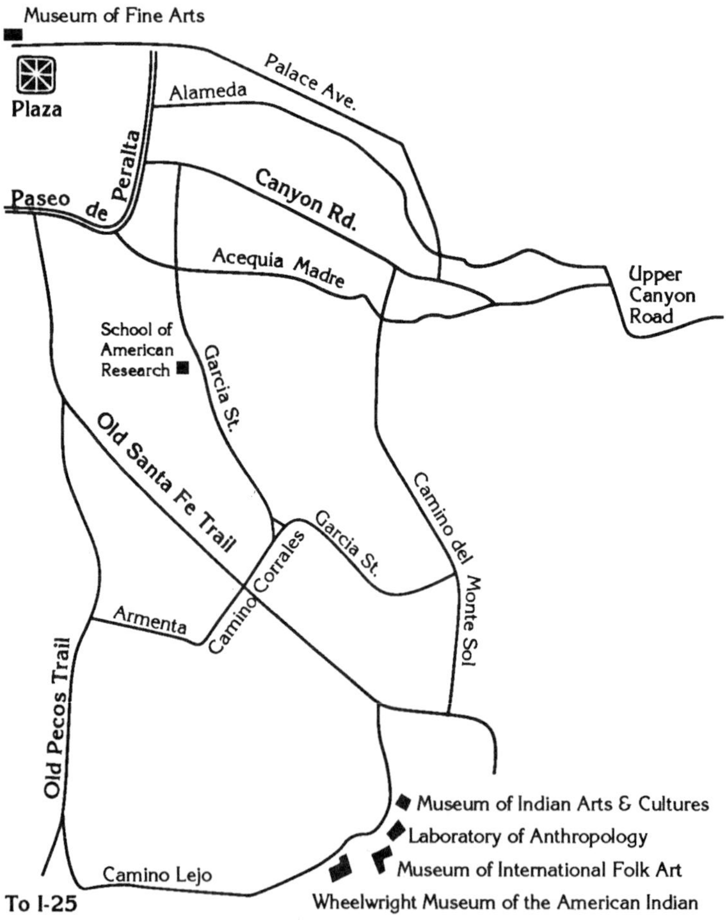

Museum of Fine Arts
Plaza
Palace Ave.
Alameda
Peralta
Paseo de
Canyon Rd.
Acequia Madre
Upper Canyon Road
School of American Research
Garcia St.
Old Santa Fe Trail
Camino del Monte Sol
Garcia St.
Camino Corrales
Armenta
Old Pecos Trail
Camino Lejo
To I-25
Museum of Indian Arts & Cultures
Laboratory of Anthropology
Museum of International Folk Art
Wheelwright Museum of the American Indian

MUSEUMS

New Mexico has collected much of its heritage in some very good museums. On the off-chance that our readers would like to see an atomic bomb or learn everything there is to know about Theodore Roosevelt's Rough Riders or admire fine paintings by the masters, we (really, Jacqueline Dunnington) have assembled what may be the only complete listing of the museums of Northern New Mexico:

SANTA FE'S MUSEUMS

The Museum of New Mexico, a statewide agency, operates four museums in Santa Fe. These museums offer the visitor a vast wealth of displays featuring arts and crafts native to the Southwest. Additionally, the Museum of New Mexico has a Statewide Services Center at 120 Lincoln Street (just north of the Plaza) which operates the Museum's programs and educational projects. The phone number is (505) 827-6480. The Museum of New Mexico also sponsors the Laboratory of Anthropology for research work at 708 Camino Lejo; the phone number there is (505) 827-8941. This laboratory facility has a few select artifacts on display but it is not a museum. The general number for the Museum of New Mexico is (505) 827-6463; a recording will inform the visitor of exhibits and programs currently offered.

Hours: 9:30 a.m.-4:45 p.m. daily in the summer; 10 a.m.-5 p.m. otherwise (except January and February when they are closed on Mondays)

Museum of Indian Arts and Culture

710 Camino Lejo
Santa Fe, New Mexico
87504
(505) 827-8941

This museum places a focus on the historical and contemporary aspects of the cultures of the native peoples of the Southwest. Not only are there permanent exhibitions of arts and crafts, but frequent demonstrations which show the manufacture of these items. This is a spectacular new building.

Museum of International Folk Art

706 Camino Lejo
Santa Fe, New Mexico 87504
(505) 827-8350

This museum presents the largest collection of folk art in the world. The new Girard Foundation collection wing is fascinating for its diversity and for its colorful and fanciful tableaux. The Folk Art Museum offers something of interest to all ages.

Museum of Fine Arts

107 West Palace Avenue
Santa Fe, New Mexico 87504
(505) 827-4452

A permanent collection of the Fine Arts museum includes the art of painters Marsden Hartley, Robert Henri, Georgia O'Keeffe, Victor Higgins, Joan Sloan and photographic works of Beaumont Newhall, Eliot Porter, Ansel Adams and others. Many major loan exhibitions are also presented here.

Palace of the Governors

105 West Palace Avenue
Santa Fe, New Mexico 87504
(505) 827-6474

The Palace of the Governors is the oldest still-standing public building in the United States; the Spanish built it between 1609 and1610. The exhibits which cover Spanish, Mexican and American eras collectively present a visual history of the Southwest.

Indian Arts Research Center at the School of American Research

660 Garcia Street
Santa Fe, New Mexico 87501
(505) 984-0742

Hours: Tour of the collection 2 p.m. Fridays

This is not strictly a display museum but a study laboratory devoted to Southwestern Indian arts and crafts. Founded in 1907, it houses the largest and most exhaustive collection of Indian pottery available, as well as textiles and paintings.

Institute of American Indian Arts

1639 Cerrillos Road
Santa Fe, New Mexico 87501
(505) 988-6281

Hours: 8 a.m.-5 p.m. Monday through Friday

The Institute of American Indian Arts operates an arts degree program (AFA) at the junior college level. Also, the institution maintains a museum of contemporary Native American art which features both a permanent collection and hosts changing shows with the works of students, faculty and prominent Native American artists from throughout the United States.

The Santa Fe Children's Museum

Armory for the Arts
1050 Old Pecos Trail
Santa Fe, New Mexico 87501

Hours: 10 a.m.-5 p.m. Thursday through Saturday
12 noon-5 p.m. Sunday

This newly-opened museum features hands-on participation in exhibits that involve the creative processes in culture, science, humanities and more. The innovative Children's Museum invites all children to discover and explore, through play and learning, the world about them. Excellent large cockroaches to handle here.

The Wheelwright Musem of the American Indian

704 Camino Lejo
Santa Fe, New Mexico 87502
(505) 982-4636

Hours: 10 a.m. -5 p.m. Monday through Saturday
1 p.m.-5 p.m. Sunday
Closed on Mondays from November 1 to March 1

The Wheelwright Museum was founded in 1937 and houses a vast collection of Navajo, Apache, Hopi and Pueblo arts and crafts. The museum states that it is "a meeting place for the recording and interpretation of the continuing traditions and creative expressions of American Indian peoples." An excellent museum shop and trading post is located on the lower floor. Very reliable and authentic Indian crafts, pawn, books, posters, weaving, etc. are sold.

Old Church Buildings as Museums in Santa Fe

Much of the culture of Northern New Mexico is derived from the religious heritage of the early settlers here. The visitor is invited to see churches, chapels, the miraculous stairway and healing sanctuarios, as well as the *moradas* of the Penitentes, because these are the structures and cultural symbols which explain who the people were who came to live here.

A few visitors are put off by the Catholicness of it all, and to them we say: the religious aspects of this region are indispensable to an understanding and appreciation of what happened here in the 17th century and since.

El Santuario de Guadalupe

100 Guadalupe Street
Santa Fe, New Mexico
87501
(505) 988-2027

Hours: 9 a.m.-3 p.m. Tuesday through Friday 10 a.m. -3 p.m. Saturday

The Santuario de Guadalupe is the oldest still-standing building in the United States dedicated to Our Lady of Guadalupe. It was built by the Franciscan missionaries at the end of the 18th century. This charming old structure now serves as a center for performing arts as well as a museum. Mass is offered at noon on the 12th of each month in remembrance of Our Lady of Guadalupe, whose feast day is December 12th.

The Loretto Chapel

211 Old Santa Fe Trail
Santa Fe, New Mexico
87501
(505) 988-5531 (hotel);
984-7971 (chapel)

Hours: 9 a.m.-5 p.m. daily

This chapel, built under the aegis of the Sisters of Loretto, was completed in 1878. Due to an error in building plans, there was no access to the choir loft, and the sisters hired a single carpenter (as a casual laborer) to execute the project. The stairway he created, which some believe is a work of miraculous intervention, has 33 stairs with no center support. No visit to Santa Fe is complete without a visit to the graceful chapel with the extraordinary staircase.

San Miguel Mission

401 Old Santa Fe Trail
Santa Fe, New Mexico 87501
(505) 983-3974

Hours: 10:30 a.m.-3:30 p.m. Monday through Saturday
1 p.m.-4:30 p.m. Sunday

Built about 1610 (at the founding of the City of Holy Faith, Santa Fe) for the Tlaxcalan (Mexican) Indian servants of the Spaniards, it has undergone many changes and reconstructions. The visitor will not only see some of the original masonry but also old beams and some fine early religious art in a chapel setting. Mass is celebrated each Sunday at 5 p.m. All documentation indicates that this is the oldest church building in the United States.

Other Museums

The College of Santa Fe, St. John's College, the ***Santa Fe Public Library*** (Washington Avenue branch), and the ***Governor's Gallery*** in the State Capitol building present frequently-changing shows of the arts, crafts, and photography of artisans from throughout New Mexico.

Abiquiu

Florence Hawley Ellis Museum of Anthropology
Ghost Ranch Museum

Abiquiu, New Mexico 87510
(505) 685-4333

Hours: 1 p.m.-5 p.m. Saturday and Sunday

This museum houses the recently-excavated anthropological materials from the Ghost Ranch Gallina digs. It also has a collection of regional arts and crafts, Pueblo Indian costumes and the skeleton of the Coelophysis dinosaur (see New Mexico State Fossil). New exhibits present tableaux of prehistoric food preparation and the steps in making pottery.

La Cienega

Old Cienega Village Museum at El Rancho de las Golondrinas

Route 14 (Exit 271 off Interstate 25 south from Santa Fe)
La Cienega, New Mexico

Mailing Address:
El Rancho de las Golondrinas
Route 14, Box 214
Santa Fe, New Mexico 87505
(505) 471-2261

El Rancho de las Golondrinas was once a stopover on the Royal Road (El Camino Real) from Mexico City to Santa Fe. This 18th century ranch offers an excellent opportunity for the museum visitor to see old mills, a threshing ground, a winery, a blacksmith's shop and other aspects of Spanish Colonial life, maintained to provide an authentic flavor not found elsewhere.

There are two festivals at the museum—the first weekend in June and the first weekend in October—and official Open House events are held the first Sundays of July, August and September. The museum is open to group tours booked well in advance, and to rentals for special events.

New Mexico's

State Animal

The Black Bear (*Oso Negro*) is the official state animal. This bear is used as the emblem of the New Mexico Department of Game and Fish. The famous "Smokey the Bear" was a black bear cub found hiding in a tree after a fire in the Lincoln National Forest, New Mexico.

Las Vegas

Antonio Sanchez Cultural Center

166 Bridge Street
Las Vegas, New Mexico 87701
(505) 454-1401, ext. 77

Hours: 9 a.m.-1 p.m. Monday through Friday
12 noon-5 p.m. Saturday
Closed Sunday and holidays

This museum presents traveling exhibits of historical interest drawn from the photo archives and artifact collections of other institutions.

Rough Riders Memorial and City Museum

727 Grand Avenue (P.O. Box 179)
Las Vegas, New Mexico 87701
(505) 425-8726

Hours: 9 a.m.-4 p.m. Monday through Saturday, closed Sunday and holidays

History lovers will enjoy this museum. Theodore Roosevelt (the 26th President) organized the Rough Riders in Las Vegas, New Mexico. Mementos and memorabilia of this episode in American history are on view. Also, many other souvenirs of local interest and Indian artifacts (including a skeleton from Pecos) enhance this collection. At a reunion of the Rough Riders here in Las Vegas, Roosevelt announced for the first time that he was a candidate for President.

Los Alamos

Bradbury Science Museum

Diamond Drive
Los Alamos, New Mexico 87544
(505) 667-4444

Hours: 9 a.m.-5 p.m. Tuesday through Friday, 1 p.m.-5 p.m. Saturday, Sunday, and Monday

The development of the first nuclear weapons during World War II is on display, and a guide is available to answer any questions. There are also exhibits showing recent advances not only in weaponry but also in scientific research in all forms of energy. A model nuclear accelerator is on view, and films are showing continuously.

Bandelier National Monument Museum

National Park Service
New Mexico Highway 4
Los Alamos, New Mexico 87544
(505) 672-3861

Hours: Summer 8 a.m.-7 p.m.
Winter 8 a.m.-5 p.m.
Closed on Christmas Day

There is a small museum in the park building in which artifacts from the Indian cultures of the area are presented with relevant history from 1200 A.D. to the present. An excellent film on the evolution of the Jemez area is shown in a small theater.

Fuller Lodge Art Center

2132 Central Avenue
Los Alamos, New Mexico 87544
(505) 662-9331

Hours: 10 a.m.-4 p.m. Monday through Saturday, 1-4 Sunday

This historic landmark designed by John Gaw Meem was once the dining and recreational facility for the Los Alamos Ranch School. A permanent collection of regional artists and travelling presentations are mounted throughout the year.

Los Alamos Historical Museum

1921 Juniper Street
Los Alamos, New Mexico
(505) 662-6272

Hours: 10 a.m.-4 p.m. Monday through Saturday, 1 p.m.-4 p.m. Sunday

Artifacts from the ancient Pajarito Plateau civilization are housed here along with photographs of the Los Alamos Ranch School. Public lectures are offered frequently on matters of local historical and cultural interest.

New Mexico's

State Flag

One of the most distinctive and colorful flags of any state in the Union, its crimson Zia sun symbol is set on a golden ground. See the section on Zia Pueblo (page 83) for a detailed history of the flag.

Madrid

Old Coal Mine Museum

New Mexico Highway 14
Madrid, New Mexico 87010
(505) 473-0743

Hours: 10 a.m.-sunset daily (weather permitting)

Mining and railroad exhibits at an authentic coal mining site. The public can readily observe a seam of coal in an old mine shaft.

Mora

Old Mill Museum

Hwy 518 (just North of town)
Mora, New Mexico
(505) 387-2654

Hours: 10 a.m.-4 p.m. Wednesday through Saturday

The last mill (flour) built in New Mexico opened in 1989 as a museum. Surprisingly intact inside and out. There is an admission fee. The La Cueva Mill is nearby.

Taos

Ernest L. Blumenschein Memorial Home

13 Ledoux Street
Taos, New Mexico 87571
(505) 758-4741

Hours: 9 a.m.-5 p.m. daily (summer)
10 a.m.-5 p.m. daily (winter)
Closed Thanksgiving, Christmas and New Year's Day

This 11-room Spanish Colonial style house contains the furnishings of the artist and his family. Changing displays of the works of local artists and craftspeople are presented throughout the year.

Governor Bent House and Museum

Bent Street
Taos, New Mexico 87571
(505) 738-2376

Hours: 9 a.m.-5 p.m. daily (summer)
10 a.m.-5 p.m. daily (winter)

This historic building, home of the first civil governor of New Mexico when it became a U.S. Territory in 1846, is furnished in the period. Bent was killed in this house during a rebellion in 1847.

La Hacienda de Don Antonio Severino Martinez

Ranchitos Road
Taos, New Mexico 87571
(505) 758-1000

Hours: 9 a.m.-5 p.m. daily (summer)
1 p.m.-5 p.m. daily (winter)
Closed Thanksgiving, Christmas and New Year's Day

This fine example of an 18th century fortified hacienda has 21 rooms and two courtyards. Call for dates of summer festivals here.

The Harwood Foundation Library and Museum (of the University of New Mexico)

25 Ledoux Street
Taos, New Mexico 87571
(505) 758-3063

Hours: 9 a.m.-5 p.m. Monday through Saturday (summer), 10 a.m.-5 p.m. Monday through Saturday (winter), closed Sunday and holidays

The permanent collection features works by the founding members of the Taos Society of Artists (established in 1915) along with other fine works. There is a good research library, other public rooms and a children's library.

Kit Carson Home and Historical Museum

East Kit Carson Road
Taos, New Mexico 87571
(505) 738-4741

Hours: 9 a.m.-5 p.m. daily (summer)
10 a.m.-5 p.m. daily (winter)
Closed Thanksgiving, Christmas and New Year's Day

The home of the famous frontier scout and mountain guide (1809-1868) contains historical items and archeological exhibits from the greater Taos area. Three rooms are furnished in the style of Kit Carson, who lived here for 25 years.

Millicent Rogers Museum

State Highway 522 (4.2 miles north of Taos)
P.O. Box A
Taos, New Mexico 87571
(505) 758-2462

Hours: 9 a.m.-5 p.m. daily (summer)
10 a.m.-4 p.m. daily (winter)
Closed Easter, San Geronimo Day (Sept. 30), Thanksgiving, Christmas and New Year's Day

This outstanding private museum has one of the finest collections in America of Indian crafts, Southwestern artifacts and Hispanic religious arts. In addition to the superb permanent collection, changing shows featuring arts of New Mexico and the Southwest are frequently presented. Group tours arranged with a 24-hour advance notice.

Nicolai Fechin House and Institute

227 North Pueblo Road
Taos, New Mexico 87571
(505) 758-1710

Hours: 1 p.m.-5:30 p.m. weekends only, from Memorial Day through September

Fechin, a Russian-American artist, built and designed this adobe house that holds fine hand-worked furniture and wooden architectural details.

Zozobra, Santa Fe's Old Man Gloom

Downtown Taos

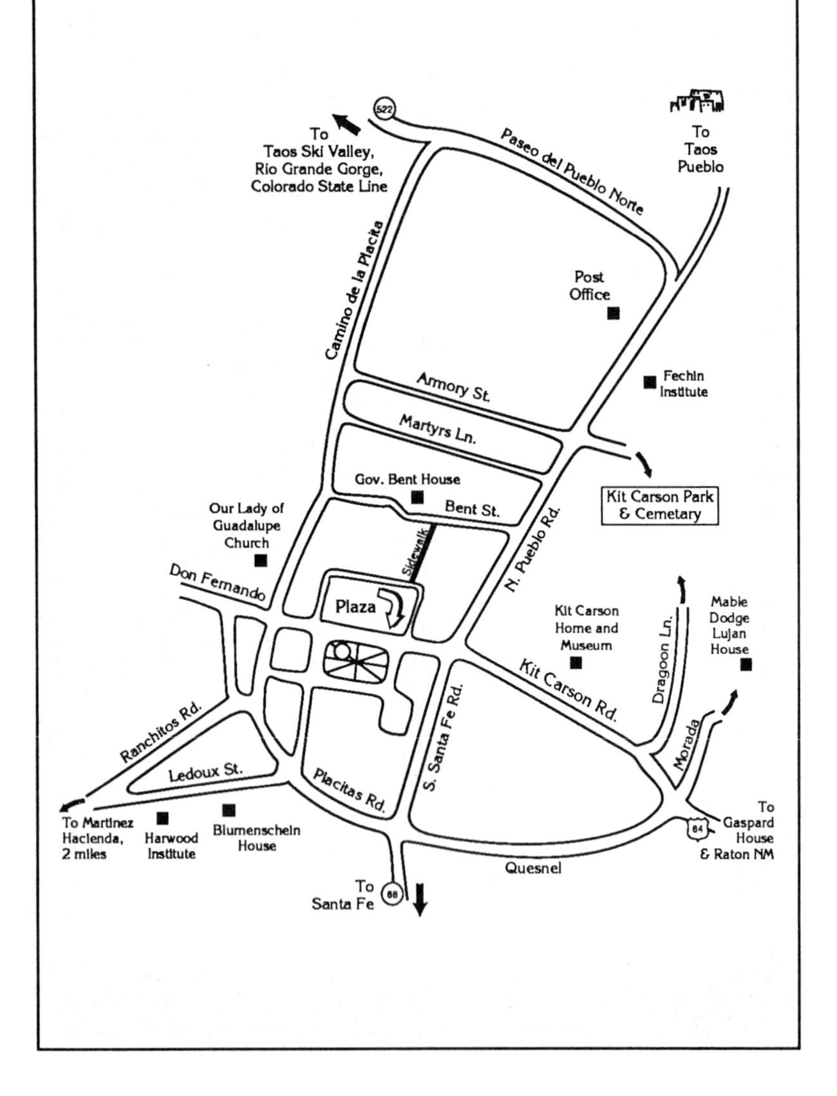

TAOS

by Jacqueline Dunnington

Taos is a small town set in one of the most dramatic landscapes in the world. The town itself is situated on a high-altitude plateau in the desert of northern New Mexico. The Rio Grande Gorge cuts deep into the land west of Taos, while to the east the rugged Sangre de Cristo Mountains form a glorious wall over which the sun rises to light the vast floor of the Taos Valley. The early Spanish explorers named these mountains "Blood of Christ" because of the full range of reddish tones cast on the mountains at sunset. The highest point in this range of the Rocky Mountains is Wheeler Peak at 13,151 feet above sea level.

Some researchers insist the name Taos (rhyme it with "house") comes from the Tiwa language, which is a member of the Native American Tanoan linguistic family. In this language it means "red willow," a variety which grows abundantly in the area and seems to take on a reddish glow in winter months. Other linguists suggest different and plausible explanations; some go as far as to include a fanciful link to Chinese. Regardless of the word Taos, it is the name of a town no visitor to New Mexico should miss. If Santa Fe has become a bit trendy and sophisticated recently, Taos is still the essence of the timeless place. A visitor's days here are inevitably marked by spectacular sunrises, with sunsets of equal grandeur. The seemingly ageless mode of life at the Taos Pueblo adds to an eerie sense of stepping out of the present time into another era.

A very brief review of the romantic history of Taos can only add to an appreciation of this most unusual town—now principally known for the arts. Most historians agree that the Taos area we know today was founded by Fray Pedro de Miranda in about 1617. If you remember your American history, this was three years before the Pilgrims arrived to establish the Plymouth Colony in Massachusetts. Certainly there had been prehistoric peoples in the area since about 3000 B.C., and Taos Pueblo was flourishing when Coronado and his band explored the environs in 1540 A.D. (See the Taos Pueblo section, page 81, for more details.) The Pueblo Revolt of 1680 sent the Spaniards back to the south shores of the Rio Grande some 370 miles away. Although the Spanish returned in 1692-93, the following century was marked by many local revolts. The Taos Valley was resettled by the Spaniards in the 18th century; all residents were under the rule of the crown of Spain until Mexican Independence in 1821. Mexican rule lasted until 1848 when the United States acquired the territory under the terms of the Treaty of Guadalupe-Hidalgo at the end of the Mexican War (1846-1848).

Curiously, the town is still officially called Don Fernando de Taos, the name by which it has been known since the 18th century. An investigation of this name leaves many questions unanswered because several men with the name Fernando or Fernandez have had links to the community. The real namesake still remains a mystery man.

In the early 19th century, trapper-traders known as "mountain men" started to infiltrate the greater Taos Mountain areas, and a new business in furs centered in Taos, in addition to the other established trading activities. By mid-century, settlers from the eastern United States arrived in covered wagons. Railroads never came into the center of the town of Taos; the only service began in 1880 and was west of the Rio Grande, on the Denver and Rio Grande Western. The nearest stop on this narrow gauge railroad was Embudo Station, nearly 20 miles southwest of town, on the west side of the deep Rio Grande Gorge.

In the 1840s, Americans from the East began to settle Taos in numbers; they set up the first "Anglo" governor, Charles Bent, who was murdered in 1847 in his Taos residence shortly after his inaugural during a brief revolution. This was the era of that famous trapper, guide and frontiersman Christopher "Kit" Carson (1809-1868). In 1912, when New Mexico Territory was admitted to statehood, Taos became legally and practically an American town. But it remains one of the most unique communities in the nation.

Taos Artists

Joseph Henry Sharp (1859-1953) is accepted as the founding father of the Taos art colony. Sharp moved to Taos in 1912, and was present at the founding of the Taos Society of Artists in July, 1915 (although 1912, 1914 and 1916 have also been given as the founding dates). There were six founding members, but the official membership has been given as 8, 10, 11 and even 21 at different dates. To be a member, the artist had to win a prize at a major show, and the other members had to approve of the artist's work. The Society was disbanded in 1927, but in those 12 years the Taos Society developed a high standard of arts for its members and brought to the public exhibits of works of the members.

Mabel Dodge Luhan, a wealthy woman born in Buffalo, N.Y., settled in Taos in 1916 after being involved with the arts in New York City's Greenwich Village. Along with the Taos Society of Artists she became a guiding force in the establishment of the town as a major arts center. Some of the famous writers who visited or lived in Taos were Willa Cather, Thornton Wilder and D. H. Lawrence (who lived here twice for a total of 18 months). The famous Swiss psychiatrist Carl Gustav Jung visited Taos Pueblo for his studies of ethnology and folk religion. Among the Taos painters were John Sloan, Randall Davey, Victor Higgins and Robert Henri.

Shops and Galleries

We advise visitors to start discovering Taos at the Plaza, in the middle of town. It was the core of the Spanish village settlement and it dates to the 18th century.

Starting along the south side of the Plaza, you will walk past *La Fonda de Taos* hotel (505/758-2211). The "only showing" of the famous D.H. Lawrence paintings of nudes (which were banned in London by Scotland Yard in 1929) hangs in the manager's office. For a dollar fee any visitor can see these works, which are sometimes signed "Lorenzo" or simply D.H. The *Fennell Art Gallery* (505/758-0749) has its showroom in the lobby of La Fonda and offers a collection of Southwestern art. Nearby, *Cowboys and Indians Collectibles* (505/758-2188) specializes in regional and Old West artifacts for purchase.

Moving west out of the Plaza area, stroll over to LeDoux Street to find the *Blumenschein Home* (505/758-0330). This is a fine spot to take your first step into the past. The historic adobe house with portions dating from the 1790s preserves the living quarters of one of the founding members of the Taos Society of Artists. *The Harwood Foundation* (505/758-3063) nearby is operated by the University of New Mexico. This is a public library, research facility, and 7,000-volume children's library in an extended, pueblo-style complex; it operates educational programs, community cultural activities and the Museum of Taos Art. The staff is most accommodating and will give you a free copy of a valuable Taos reading list.

The *Tally Richards Gallery* (505/758-2731) on LeDoux Street represents the work of outstanding contemporary artists. On the same street is R. C. Gorman's *Navajo Gallery* (505/758-3250) which has a full display of the artist's work. R. C. Gorman is a resident of Taos.

Wander back through streets lined with adobe houses to the north side of the Plaza where the art galleries, restaurants and shops wait to tempt you. *Artwears* (505/758-8850) sells outstanding contemporary jewelry with many pieces handmade. *New Directions Gallery* (505/758-2771) features new artistic talent. *Burke Armstrong* (505/758-9016) and *Bryans Gallery* (505/758-9407) offer the visitor fine arts of lasting value.

Moving north out of the Plaza area, walk to famous Bent Street on the west side of the main street (here called Paseo del Pueblo Norte). Drop into *Indigo Kitchen* (505/758-3126) for a gourmet need, pick up a book at *Moby Dickens Bookshop* (505/758-3050), have that first lunch at the *Apple Tree Restaurant* (505/758-1900). Many other shops await you on this famous short street.

Don't miss a stop at the *Governor Bent House and Museum* (505/758-2376). Home of New Mexico's first American governor, early trader, trapper and mountain man, the Governor Bent Museum and Gallery of Western Art is housed in Charles Bent's old adobe home on Bent Street. In 1846, Bent was appointed governor of New Mexico when the state became American territory during the Mexican War. In 1847, he was killed by an angry mob protesting American rule. The Governor Bent House is the scene of his death. Today, the museum displays furniture and Western and Indian artifacts.

The portion of Paseo del Pueblo Norte north of Taos Plaza is a treasure trove of local culture. On the west side, *Weaving/Southwest* (505/758-0433) specializes in the tapestry work of 20 local artists from the three cultures. *Fenix Gallery* (505/758-9120) represents many outstanding local contemporary artists. On the opposite side of the road, the *Hensley Gallery Southwest* has been offering fine art, with many traditional works, since 1967. The *Taos Traditions Gallery* (505/758-0016) features works of contemporary artists. *The Stables Art Center* (505/758-2036) in the *Stables Art Gallery* offers changing exhibitions of the artists of New Mexico. This is also the home address (133 Paseo del Pueblo

Norte, Taos, NM 87571) for the Taos Art Association.

Going east from Taos Plaza is the Kit Carson Road area with its abundance of shops, galleries, places to eat and browse, all set in a historically important part of Taos. *DEL Fine Art* (505/758-1131), on the north side of the road, offers a collection of some of the most prominent names in the world of contemporary art. Next door is the *Kit Carson Home and Museum* which is a tourist "must."

In 1843, Kit Carson, the famous Indian scout, purchased this home as a wedding gift for his bride, Josefa Jaramillo. This 12-room house, featuring 30-inch adobe walls, houses the Kit Carson Museum. Three of the rooms are furnished as they might have been when Kit Carson and his family lived there for 25 years. The remaining rooms include the Carson Room, the Spanish Room and the Early American Room.

Across the street, on the south side, is *El Rincón* (505/758-9188), a trading post, curio shop and private museum all in one. The history of Taos is visually presented to the visitor along with an opportunity to collect fine pawn silver and turquoise items. The *Taos Bookshop* (505/758-3733), the oldest bookshop in New Mexico, has collected superb first editions, out-of-print materials and works of best-selling authors.

Exploring Taos

Taos Walking Tours (505/758-3861) will guide you around Taos daily from June 1 through the end of September. The tour leaves the Kit Carson Home and Museum at 10 a.m. If you visit between October 1 and the end of May, a tour by special appointment readily can be booked.

Pride of Taos operates an in-town trolley service daily, which departs from the Taos Plaza to serve all the hotels/motels north and south of this central area. For hours, call 505/758-8340.

At the end of a day spent on foot investigating Taos, a refreshing drink at the *Historic Taos Inn* on Paseo Pueblo del Norte offers an opportunity to visit this famous meeting place.

Automobile trips outside the downtown area will round out the Taos experience, since many points of interest are spread over the entire valley area.

Southwest of Taos, on Ranchitos Road, is *La Hacienda de Don Severino Martinez* (505/758-1000). A visit to this early fortified hacienda can be readily combined with a drive to Ranchos de Taos. The Martinez Hacienda, with its thick adobe walls, no outside windows and 21 rooms opening on two courtyards, is of the 1804-1827 Spanish Colonial period. There are festivals at the Martinez house during the summer. Call for exact dates.

At the beginning of Ranchitos Road is the *Milagro de Taos Gallery* (505/758-2111); it features an outstanding collection of folk art.

In the opposite direction, north off Kit Carson Road, is *La Morada de Don Fernando de Taos*. It is open to the public by appointment only (505/758-4741)—through the Kit Carson Foundation. Extensive research facilities and archives are here for students of Southwestern lore. The building once served as a Penitente Brotherhood chapel. (The Penitentes of New Mexico are a religious fraternity with roots in Spain, which provided Catholic religious activity when the Spanish priests left Nuevo Mexico. During the Mexican era the Penitente *moradas* were the center of a folk religion here.)

Driving north from the Taos Plaza, the first stop we suggest is a quick tour of the *Kit Carson Park and Cemetery* fronting the east side of the main street, Paseo del Pueblo Norte. Carson is buried in an area adjacent to the large recreational facility. Next stop might be the *Fechin Institute* (505/758-1710). Home to the Russian-born painter, Nicolai Fechin, this traditional Southwestern adobe features handcarved doors, windows and gates mixed with features found in a typical Russian country home. Built in 1928 the house and adjacent studio were home to the internationally renowned artist. The house has been listed on the National Register of Historic Places since 1979. The institute is a cultural-education center dedicated to Fechin's unique approach to learning, teaching and creativity. Fechin's own personal collection of art, as well as the work of other artists, is displayed periodically. Hours vary seasonally.

The *Overland Sheepskin Company* (505/758-8822), three miles north of Taos on the right side of Highway 522, is just the spot to purchase that wonderful bit of sheepskin clothing or bedding. This shop, now with branches in many areas, offers rustic couture at its best, from 8 a.m. to 8 p.m. daily.

Four miles north of town, just southwest of "the blinking light," is the world-famous *Millicent Rogers Museum* (505/758-2462). The museum was established in memory of Millicent Rogers, a Standard Oil heiress who settled in Taos in 1947. The core of the permanent collection is an extensive display of the finest in Southwestern folk art, jewelry, textiles and pottery. The museum also presents changing exhibitions, tours of the collection and educational activities.

A drive west on Highway U.S. 64 takes the tourist to the *Rio Grande Gorge Bridge*; at 650 feet above the river, it is the highest bridge in the United States. When it was completed in 1965, it linked the western side of the gorge to the greater Taos area from which it had been isolated.

Fifteen miles northwest of Taos on Highway 522, in San Cristobal, is the *D. H. Lawrence Ranch and Shrine*. The famous author and his wife, Freida, lived here at various times from 1922 to 1925 for a total of 18 months. His remains are mixed into the mortar of the shrine. The ranch was a present from Mabel Dodge Luhan to Freida Lawrence. It is now owned by the University of New Mexico.

THE SEASONS

The seasonal changes in Taos present the visitor with a variety of special cultural and sporting opportunities, and the need to plan accordingly.

Winter

In the winter, there can be more than 100 inches of dry, powder snow in the Ski Valley. The town of Taos has a much lighter snowfall, but every winter sees its share of snow-edged adobe houses in the village. Winter clothing is a must, as are goggles for skiing and sunglasses for touring, due to the brilliant sun; boots (not city shoes) are called for in the area. In addition to downhill skiing, the Taos area offers cross-country skiing, snowmobiling and some winter fishing. In some resort hotels, there is indoor swimming and even tennis. Special events at Taos Pueblo contribute to an enchanting Christmas season, an ideal time to elect a vacation in Taos.

Spring

Spring comes to Taos by late April and whitewater rafting starts then on the headwaters of the Rio Grande. The massive snowmelt generated in the Sangre de Cristo Mountains provides turbulent waters to suit the most daring rafter. Rafting can be booked through *Big River Raft Trips* (505/758-3204 or 505/471-5636), *Far Flung Adventures* (505/758-2628), *Los Rios River Runners* (505/758-1550) or *Rio Grande Rapid Transit* (505/758-9700). The Rio Grande is usually too wild for spring fishing and the angler is advised to head for smaller streams or Eagle Nest Lake. In late spring (late May-early June) there is a Spring Arts Festival in town and Taos Pueblo openly invites guests to the dances they present. (See Taos Pueblo, page 81.)

Summer

Taos enjoys a glorious summer with warm sunny days and cool evenings. Glider buffs can enjoy a Soaring Fiesta in mid-June, rodeo lovers witness the Rodeo de Taos in late June and the town of Taos celebrates Fiestas de Taos in late July. Throughout the summer, it is wise to check the events at Taos Pueblo and to attend a performance in the Taos School of Music's chamber series. Hikers can take to the Carson National Forest all year around, but summer is the time to see the flora. It is essential for the mountaineer to bring along warm clothing and emergency provisions in the backpack because the weather can be fickle at the higher elevations; check in with the Ranger District in the area of your choice for details or warnings. The Carson National Forest Ranger District Offices are:

Canjilon Ranger District
P.O. Box 488
Canjilon, NM 87515
505/ 684-2486

El Rito Ranger District
P.O. Box 56
El Rito, NM 87530
505/581/4554

Jicarilla Ranger District
Gobernador Route
Blanco, NM 87412
505/326-2036

Camino Real Ranger District
15160 State Road 75
P.O. Box 68
Penasco, NM 87553

Tres Piedras Ranger District
P.O. Box 728
Tres Piedras, NM 87577
505/758-8678

Questa Ranger District
P.O. Box 110
Questa, NM 87556
505/586-0520

Taos Pueblo invites you to several annual summer events, fish are jumping, galleries are open and the tourist has a wide choice of diversions. Sunglasses, sun block cream, a hat and your camera should be with you.

Fall

The autumn season offers the hunter ample sport, shooting small and big game: dove, pigeon, grouse, wild turkey, elk, deer, cougar and more. Licenses and permits, limited in some instances, are required and can be had at most sporting goods shops or through the New Mexico Department of Game and Fish, Villagra Building, Santa Fe, NM (505/827-7880). The mountains are aglow with leaves turning to gold in one of the largest aspen stands in the United States. Taos Pueblo celebrates its patron, San Geronimo, and in the town of Taos a Festival of the Arts provides a wonderful chance for the tourist to enjoy the art scene. Sweaters and jackets are needed in the fall; the altitude is 6,950 feet above sea level.

Climate Statistics for the Town of Taos

Annual average snowfall: 24 inches
Annual average rainfall: 12 inches
Average January temperature: 10°F to 40°F
Average July temperature: 50°F to 88°F

WHERE TO FIND HELP

Taos may seem to be in a realm beyond time; however, there are state-of-the-art emergency services available to the visitor. A few important numbers are:

Police (Town of Taos) 758-2216
N.M. State Police 758-8878
Taos County Sheriff 758-3361
Fire, Taos and environs 758-2201
Ambulance, Taos 758-9591 or 758-1911

Taos has had a community hospital for more than 50 years, Holy Cross Hospital on Paseo del Pueblo Sur/South Santa Fe Road (758-8883). There is not only 24-hour emergency care at this facility, but also the services of 19 staff doctors. For the most acute cases there is ground or helicopter service to the major medical centers in Albuquerque, including the University of New Mexico's outstanding trauma and burn units.

The tourist can turn to the Taos County Chamber of Commerce (800/732-TAOS or in New Mexico 505/758-3873) for requests for specialized information. Taos Central Reservations (800/821-2437 or in New Mexico 505/758-9767) is of invaluable help in securing lodgings, especially during the ski season. *The Taos News*, a local weekly newspaper, informs the visitor of current happenings, as does *The Sangre de Cristo Chronicle*.

GETTING THERE

The Taos Plaza is 68 miles north of the Santa Fe Plaza by automobile. The most direct route is via U.S. Highways 84/285 into Española, and then north on Highway 68 to Taos along the Rio Grande, a very scenic route. Because there is no rail service, transportation to Taos is by wheels or wings (unless you are a career hiker). Mesa Airlines (800/637-2247, or in New Mexico 505/758-9677) provides regular if sometimes erratic service from the Albuquerque International Airport to the Taos Airport twice daily except Saturday, when there is one flight. (Mesa sometimes takes off early, so check in well ahead of scheduled departure.) During the ski season, additional weekend flights are available on Mesa. The adult round-trip tickets start at about $65 for reservations booked well ahead. From Albuquerque, the Taos Limousine Service (800/433-1321, or in New Mexico 505/758-3524/1085) charges $140 per person for the nearly-three-hour drive. Also, Faust's Transportation Service (800/345-3738, or in New Mexico 505/758-3410) operates a shuttle service for $45 round-trip or $25 one-way. Reservations at least a day ahead are required. Greyhound-Trailways offers public bus service (800/531-5332, or in New Mexico 505/758-1144). Many visitors who enter the state by plane at Albuquerque avail themselves of the many car rental services offered. All rates quoted here are, of course, subject to the carrier's changes.

By private plane, land at Taos Municipal Airport (505/758-4995) which has Unicom (122.8) and FBO; Century Aviation (505/758-9501) Aviation gas and jet-A available. Charter service, single and multi-engine. Tie-downs, maintenance and lighted 5,800-foot runway available. Elevation: 7,091 feet.

WHERE TO EAT

The Chamber of Commerce in Taos suggests a long list of restaurants covering all price ranges and cuisines. A few of the most popular eating spots are the favorites we list. We've left out hotel dining, but some Taos hotels also have outstanding facilities.

A delightful way to introduce yourself to dining in Taos is a first meal at the charming *Apple Tree Restaurant* situated one block north of the Plaza on Bent Street (505/758-1900). Once an old house, the ground floor rooms are now a series of cozy dining areas with crackling fires in the winter and patio dining under the trees in warm weather. The menu includes a blend of innovative cooking with classic New Mexican regional fare; breads and desserts are all made on the premises; beer and wine service. Open every day for breakfast, luncheon or dinner from 8:00 a.m. to 9:30 p.m. Most major credit cards are accepted and reservations are recommended.

Another rewarding choice for good dining is at the *Brett House Restaurant* located in the historic house of the late Dorothy Brett, a Taos artist. Situated a little over three miles north of Taos on Highway 522 (505/776-8545), at the "blinking light," the restaurant boasts spectacular views of the Sangre de Cristo Mountains. The food is American-Continental with all items from appetizers to desserts prepared in the kitchens from the freshest produce. The piñon tart is a "must" dessert. An extensive beer and wine list is available. Luncheon is served daily from 11:30 a.m. (summer only) and dinner from 6 p.m. to 9:30 p.m. except Mondays. Most major credit cards are accepted and reservations should be made in advance. (In the past, the restaurant was also known as "Whitey's.")

Casa Cordova "featuring the delicacy of wild mushrooms" is another popular dining spot located about 10 miles north of Taos in Arroyo Seco (505/776-2200). Drive north out of the center of Taos on Highway 522 and then right (north) on Highway 150 (also known as the Ski Valley Road). The menu offers Northern Italian dishes along with exotic local game specialties; all this is served with a gracious flair for service and the music of a troubador. Open for dinner only from 6 p.m. and cocktails are available from 4:30 p.m. on. Closed Sunday. Most major credit cards are accepted and, as with all the premier restaurants of Taos, reservations are recommended.

For an authentic New Mexican meal in a relaxed setting, we recommend *Casa de Valdez* about two miles south of the Taos Plaza on Paseo Pueblo Sur/ South Santa Fe Road (505/758-8777). The barbeque is legendary and has been mentioned in the New York Times, the San Francisco Chronicle and other papers. A beer-wine list is excellent and the service friendly. This restaurant is open from 11 a.m. to 9:30 p.m. daily except Wednesday and Sunday, when luncheon is omitted. Most major credit cards are accepted and reservations are suggested.

The *Stakeout* offers the best in prime rib, marinated lamb, sizzling steaks and fresh seafood. High above the valley in an awesome setting, the views are said to be more than 100 miles. This informal yet luxuriously rugged restaurant is eight miles south of the Taos Plaza and is clearly marked with a cowboy hat sign (505/758-2042). Open nightly from 5:30 p.m. to 10 p.m. The visitor might well want to enjoy drinks in the lounge and bar before dining. Visa and Mastercard accepted and reservations are in order for this popular restaurant.

For those who elect to spend most of a day walking about the Taos Plaza area and gallery hopping, there is *Roberto's* (505/758-2434) which is run by the Garcia family. Regional dishes are featured at this inexpensive but authentic restaurant located across from the Kit Carson Museum. The ambiance is rustic and the service friendly. Don't be surprised to find a handwritten note taped to the front door—"Gone skiing, see you tomorrow." It is best to call ahead. Beer and wine available. Luncheons from 12 noon to 3:00 p.m., dinner from 5 p.m. to 9:00 p.m. Closed Tuesdays. Most major credit cards accepted.

Enjoy a meal at *El Patio de Taos* (505/758-2121) in the oldest building in Taos which is hidden in the alley off the northwestern corner of the Plaza. The Pueblo Indians built this outpost which later served as Governor Bent's office and was visited by Kit Carson and Buffalo Bill Cody. Continental and regional fare on a varied menu are served in this step-back-in-time restaurant. Open for luncheon from 11:30 a.m. to 3:30 p.m., for *tapas* from 4 p.m. and dinner from 5:30 p.m. until closing. Closed Sunday. Most major credit cards are accepted; reservations encouraged.

Other Popular Taos Restaurants:

Chile Connection (505/776-8787) About five miles north of Taos. Dinner only; open daily. Most credit cards. Bar service. A popular night spot.

Don Pedro's (505/758-9281) South of the Plaza about three miles. Luncheon and dinner; closed Monday. Mastercard and Visa. Beer and wine served. Mexican and American cooking.

El Taoseno (505/758-9511) South of Plaza about 2 miles. Breakfast, luncheon, dinner; open daily. No credit cards. No bar service. Family dining.

Floyd's Restaurant (505/758-4142) South of Plaza about two miles. Breakfast, luncheon, dinner; open daily. No credit cards. Bar and good service.

Garden Restaurant (505/758-9483) On the Taos Plaza. Breakfast, luncheon, dinner; open daily. Most major credit cards. Beer and wine served.

La Cocina de Taos (505/758-2412) On the Taos Plaza. Breakfast, luncheon, dinner; open daily. Most major credit cards. Bar service. Popular local spot.

La Ultima (505/758-3340) Across from the Safeway south of Plaza. Luncheon, dinner; open daily. Mastercard and Visa. Beer and wine served. Regional cooking only.

Michael's Kitchen (505/758-4178). On the main street a bit north of Plaza. Breakfast, luncheon, dinner; closed holidays. Mastercard and Visa. No bar service. Located in a local bakery.

Ogelvie's (505/758-8866) On the Taos Plaza. Luncheon, dinner; open daily. Most major credit cards. Bar service. A branch of a premier chain in the state.

Sam's Smokehaus (505/758-2357) Three blocks south of Taos Plaza. Open fro 11 a.m. to 9 p.m. Tuesday through Saturday; luncheon only on Sunday; closed Monday. Mastercard and Visa. Beer and wine served. Wonderful barbeque.

There are three meals-on-wheels services in Taos. None has bar service nor takes credit cards. They serve inexpensive luncheons only and operate in the downtown area south of the Taos Plaza. *Mante's Chow Cart* has a full range of regional dishes. The tacos are superb. *The Burrito Wagon* serves burritos that the local gourmets claim are the best this side of paradise. *Taco Bueno* does a prize-winning job with the taco. Watch for these extraordinary operations alongside the highway.

WHERE TO STAY

Bed and Breakfast

Bed-and-breakfast inns are in good supply in Taos; the Chamber of Commerce lists nearly 30 in its newest folder. Several near the Taos Plaza offer fine accommodations. *The Suite Retreat* (505/758-3960) is 2-1/2 blocks from the Plaza and offers private suites with full baths and gourmet breakfasts starting at $70 per night. *The Brooks Street Inn* (505/758-1489) was selected by Country Inns Magazine as one of the 10 best of North America; it is three blocks north of the Plaza and the rates start at $45 for a stay in a house with adobe walls and a lovely garden. The elegant *Casa de las Chimeneas* (505/758-4777) offers the tourist gourmet breakfasts and a room with its own fireplace starting at $95 the night. *La Posada de Taos* (505/758-8164) is a provincial adobe inn 2-1/2 blocks from the Plaza which features a honeymoon house—rates start at $46 the night. For those who enjoy history, a stay at the *Mabel Dodge Luhan House* (505/758-9456) which is three blocks from the Plaza would be a treat. Starting at $60, the visitor can enjoy a night where D. H. Lawrence and Georgia O'Keeffe stayed. This rambling hacienda is sometimes booked for conferences, so call well ahead for reservations.

The visitor who wants to enjoy the country near Taos should consider one among the following comfortable bed-and-breakfast facilities. *Hacienda del Sol* (505/758-0287) is a mile north of the Plaza in the country estate of Mabel Dodge Luhan. This lovely adobe features the fabulous views of Taos Mountain, a jacuzzi and a storybook garden with apple trees over 100 years old. Rates start at $45. Another excellent choice is the *Laughing Horse Inn* (505/758-8350) located a mile north of the Plaza, in a 100-year-old adobe. Your hosts offer VCR service and an extensive audio/video library. Rates start at about $39 the night. West of the Plaza, *Casa Europa Inn and Gallery* (505/758-9798) awaits the visitor with its white interior walls hung with artwork. Gourmet breakfasts are featured and rates start at $60 the night. The *Bed and Breakfast Inn - Taos* (505/758-7477) has three lovely suites in an adobe house plus *casitas* with their own kitchens; rates start at $60 but there are substantial discounts off-season. The *Chili Azul* (505/758-8841) is about three miles north of the Plaza. Two rooms are available in this private home (of an artist) and the rates start at $45 the night.

Hotels and Motels

Taos offers the traveling public many beds from which to select lodgings appropriate to purse and taste. These accommodations vary from quaint to luxurious, from town to mountain locations. *The Holiday Inn/Don Fernando de Taos* (800/HOLIDAY, or in New Mexico 505/758-4444) on South Santa Fe Road/Paseo del Pueblo Sur is the newest addition to the lodgings in Taos. There are 126 spacious rooms and suites, a large heated pool, tennis court, hot tub and conference rooms. This new resort complex is built in the tradition of the legendary Don Fernando Hotel of the 1920s which burned down in 1933. Daily rates start at $84. Also, south of the Taos Plaza and on the same road is the landmark *Sagebrush Inn* (800/428-3626, or in New Mexico 505/758-2254). The old part of this adobe inn was built in 1929 in the Pueblo-Mission style and the new addition, Sagebrush Village, offers spacious family lodging for rent or purchase. Georgia O'Keeffe once lived and painted here. The resort offers tennis courts, outdoor heated pool, patio dining and convention facilities. Rates upon request. In the same general area the traveler will find the *Sun God Lodge* (505/758-3162). The comfortable lodgings here are moderately priced starting at $35 daily, and the amenities include cable TV, outdoor picnic grounds and a hot tub. *The Quality Inn* (800/228-5151, or in New Mexico 505/758-2200) is on the same road as the four prior listings, and offers in the modest price range rooms and suites in contemporary Southwestern style and a heated pool.

At Frontier Road and Paseo del Pueblo Sur/South Santa Fe Road, only minutes south of the Taos Plaza, the *Ramada Inn* (800/2-RAMADA, or in New Mexico 505/758-2900) offers a heated pool, whirlpool spa and convention facilities. The 124 rooms feature contemporary Southwestern decor, and a cozy lounge and restaurant on the premises.

The *Hotel La Fonda de Taos* (505/758-2211) is a historic landmark and the only lodging right on the Taos Plaza. The banned paintings of D. H. Lawrence are here for all to see along with authentic New Mexican decorative arts and rugs. La Fonda is within walking distance of many shops, museums and galleries in a quaint setting free of modern glitz—a step into the past.

Quail Ridge Inn (800/624-4448, or in New Mexico 505/776-2211) is situated seven miles north of Taos on Highway 150 (known also as the Ski Valley Road). This outstanding resort and conference center offers 110 rooms and suites, 8 tennis courts, 4 racketball courts, fully-equipped kitchens, heated pool, sauna, hot tubs and more. Here the traveler finds he or she is in a complex of modern elegance which includes the majestic scenery. *Carl's French Quarter* restaurant (505/776-8319), New Orleans cooking in one of the area's newest gourmet havens. Breakfast is served from 7 p.m. to 9:30 a.m. and dinner from 5:30 p.m. to 9 p.m.; Sunday brunch is a treat. A fine wine list and bar services await the guest and most major credit cards are accepted. Try to reserve ahead.

West of Taos Plaza by four blocks is *El Monte Lodge* (505/758-3171) in a park setting. Guests enjoy adobe rooms, kiva fireplaces and kitchenettes in traditional Taos ambiance. The *Historic Taos Inn* (800/TAOS INN, or in New Mexico 505/758-2233), a step or so north of the Taos Plaza on the main street, advertises "...an adventure for visitors, a tradition for locals...." Parts of this 40-room inn date to the 17th century and the building is now in the National Register of Historic Places; the appointments are all in the Taos-Pueblo style, but modern amenities such as TV, heated pool and hot tub have been skillfully incorporated in the traditional setting. *Doc Martin's Restaurant* (505/758-2233) is just off the main lobby. The menu features New American and New Mexican cuisine. Open daily for breakfast, luncheon and dinner—reservations are wise; patio dining in warm weather.

El Pueblo Lodge (800/433-9610, or 505/758-8641 in New Mexico), five blocks north of the Plaza, invites the tourist to enjoy 48 rooms finished in Southwestern style plus heated swimming pool, hot tub, cable TV and many rooms with kitchenettes. Room rates start at $45. A comfortable place for a family with children.

The *Kachina Lodge* (800/528-1234, or in New Mexico 758-2275) is your Best Western host in the heart of Taos. The spacious 122-room inn has most resort amenities with special orientation to family service, with children under 12 free. Room rates start at $65. Conventions are welcome and dining facilities on the premises offer " . . . sumptuous or simple."

Other Lodgings

(Consult the section in this guide "Where to Find Help" to obtain general information on lodgings of all types.)

The Taos Valley R.V. Park (800/323-6009, or in New Mexico 505/758-4469) fronts the South Santa Fe Road/Paseo Pueblo del Sur Road. It is open all year and has 29 units for the RV traveler. The campground has a convenience store, laundromat, telephones, restrooms and showers and 30/50 AMP service. The rates, at present, are from $11 to $16 nightly.

The Dasburg House and Studio (505/758-2031) awaits the discriminating individual guest or a business needing a premier house rental. This classic adobe hacienda, once the home and studio of the famous Taos artist Andrew Dasburg (1887-1979), has been awarded the New Mexico Historical Marker. The luxuries here include a five-acre setting with sweeping views of the Sangre de Cristo Mountains, eight fireplaces, hot tub; daily maid service and cook by arrangement. The house holds from two to 14. For further information about booking, write the Manager, Dasburg Houe and Studio, Box 1813, Taos, New Mexico 87571. The rates are near $125 the day. A vacation in this enchanting place is a total experience of the Taos essence and not just a tourist stop.

TAOS PUEBLO

We have presented a brief overview of the Taos Pueblo in the PUEBLOS section, but deeper coverage of the pueblo will help the visitor to understand this timeless community. Taos Pueblo is one of the most photographed spots on earth; further, its powerful impact will leave lasting impressions on any tourist.

Anthropologists and other scholars present various dates for the arrival of peoples at the Taos Pueblo; the most widely accepted date for the construction of the multiple-family dwelling seen today, on the south side of the pueblo, is circa 1450 A.D. Certainly there were other pueblo settlements in the area many centuries earlier. Where did the Taos Pueblo peoples come from? To date, nobody can say for sure; perhaps they are descendants of the mysterious (now extinct) Anasazi—"the old ones" in Navajo (from the Four Corners region). Maybe they came from the plains area; students of linguistic history find many shared words/sounds at Taos Pueblo with the Kiowas now living in Oklahoma. Religious tradition has it that "the people" emerged from Blue Lake, northeast of Taos, high in the mountains.

The Taos Pueblo architectural complex is often called the oldest American apartment building because of its stacked units and shared walls. The pueblo looks today, as far as we can tell, the way it did four and a half centuries ago when Coronado saw it in 1540. These "townhouses" are constructed of sun-baked adobe. The Indians, prior to the advent of the Spanish, did not mold their adobe (mud mortar reinforced with bits of straw) into brick but used the construction material in loose or bulk form. The basic adobe walls are reinforced with interior poles. Both interior and exterior roofs are of long timbers called *vigas*, which are set in parallel rows with small sticks (*latias*) set crossways; the spaces are filled in with twigs, then adobe. The domed baking ovens, *hornos*, outside the housing clusters are also of adobe.

After the arrival of the Spaniards in 1540, Taos Pueblo entered Western history. During the famous Pueblo Revolt of 1680, all the Spanish settlers, leaders and missionaries were forced to leave the upper Rio Grande corridor and reside in the area of El Paso del Norte (now Ciudad Juarez—not quite present-day El Paso, Texas). The revolt was led by Popé, an Indian from San Juan Pueblo living in Taos Pueblo. After the revolt, this Indian leader failed to rally the scattered Indians into a viable union, thus paving the way for the successful De Vargas-led return by the Spaniards in 1692-93.

After the reconquest, the Spaniards gave the Indians farming and pasture property under a land grant program. But Indian-Spanish strife was a recurring feature of life in New Mexico in the 18th and 19th centuries. In 1847, after the arrival of east coast "Anglo" Americans, the Spanish, Mexican and Indian Taosenos joined in a local rebellion against the U.S. Government in which the first Governor of the area, Charles Bent, was murdered. The U.S. Army, in a countermove, attacked the pueblo and killed 150 Indians and some other rebels. Some of these slain natives are still considered martyrs by the Taos Pueblo. To the left of the entrance to the pueblo is the ruin of a church where many of the rebels were trapped and killed.

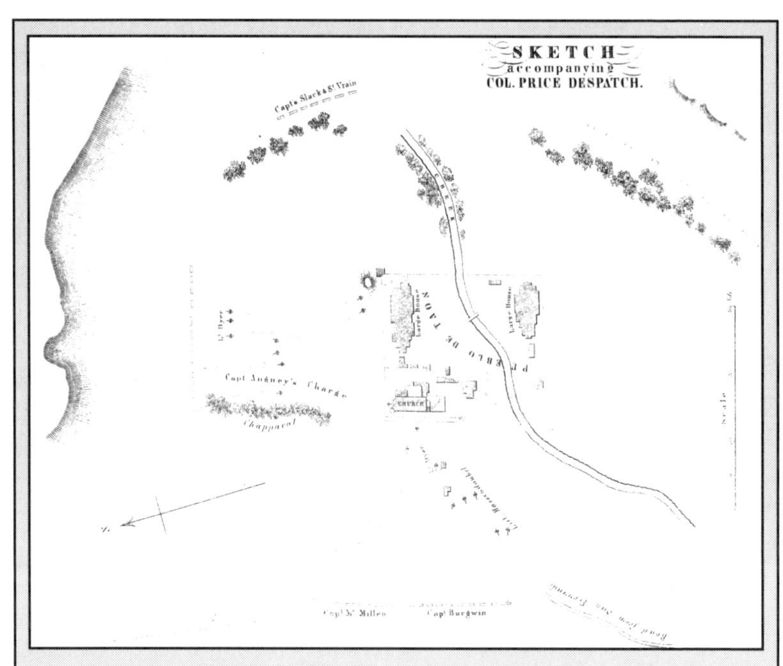

This is a sketch of the battle which accompanied Colonel Price's dispatch describing his victory over the rebels.

There is a restored cavalry fort, named after the Captain Burgwin whose troops held the west flank in this sketch. The fort is located on the south side of Highway 518, about six miles east of Ranchos de Taos. At present, it is a summer campus for Southern Methodist University. When built it was a U.S. cavalry outpost to protect the "back road" from Taos to Santa Fe from the raiding forays of the Comanche tribe.

The population of Taos Pueblo in 1989 is about 1,100, according to tribal officials. Most residents are trilingual: Tiwa, Spanish, English. The pueblo is governed by a council of 50—all men. The communal motto "Let us move evenly together" reveals an underlying philosophy of government by unanimous voice rather than by the majority rule which is typical of American-style democracy. None of the four chief leaders of Taos Pueblo is elected; each is appointed by the male elders. Prior to becoming a leader, a man must have been initiated into the secret kiva-centered religion. This philosophy of religion holds to a belief, among other views, of the sacred unity of all life. (However, being a vegetarian is not part of the Taos Pueblo tradition as it would be in other "unity of life" belief systems such as Hinduism or Buddhism.) There are six kivas at Taos Pueblo; none is open to the public—ever.

The residents of Taos Pueblo have distinctive dress which is worn for most special occasions, and regularly by some older people. Before the arrival of the Spaniards, Taos Indians wore clothing of prepared animal hide, and their footwear was a flat-heeled moccasin with hard soles and soft uppers. Due to the inhospitable climate of northern New Mexico, cotton couldn't be raised. Woven cotton cloth was obtained by barter with Indians from warmer zones, and cotton blankets became a part of the pueblo's traditional garb. The Spaniards brought sheep to the New World, and after their arrival woolen cloth was woven from the shearlings. Men of the pueblo continue to wrap a blanket around their body in winter and drape it from the waist during the warmer season. The women draw shawls around themselves. Some anthropologists maintain that the custom of wrapping in a blanket is not a very old tradition—less than a 100 years. Both sexes wear jewelry sparingly. Men bind their hair into two braids, and women draw their hair into a bundle at the back of the head.

The residents of Taos Pueblo have stalwartly tried to preserve their traditional customs in face of two waves of conquering, dominant cultures: the Spanish in the 17th century and the "Anglo" American in the 19th century. Indeed, some of the peoples of this pueblo are in the mainstream of modern culture: they drive automobiles, live in modern housing, and shop at local markets. Occupants of the pueblo exclude electricity and underground utilities for traditional reasons. And some traditional ways are retained in the family-oriented and conservative community at Taos Pueblo. For example, all the ceremonies except the purely Christian (Catholic) events at the Christmas season are expressions of the Indian cultural heritage, even if these rituals mark events in the Christian calendar. The harvest season coincides with the annual two-day celebration of the Feast of San Geronimo (St. Jerome), the patron saint of the pueblo, on September 29 an 30. During these festivities, a pueblo religious society, the "Black Eyes," performs clown-like acts which have spiritual meaning and are not to be taken as mere comic antics. In honor of San Geronimo, the other events include traditional foot races, a trade fair, ritual pole climbing and the Sundown Dance on the eve of the feast.

These Taos Pueblo public events are held on dates which are fixed. But remember to call in advance (505/758-9593) for precise details and hours.

January 1	Dances in honor of New Year's Day—Turtle Dance
January 6	King's Day dances—animal dances
February 2	Dances in honor of Candelaria (Candlemas, or the Feast of Purification)
May 3	Feast of Santa Cruz—foot race and corn dance
June 13	Feast of San Antonio—corn dance
June 24	Feast of San Juan—corn dance
July, 2nd weekend	Taos Pueblo Pow-wow
July 25	Feast of Santiago—various dances
July 26	Feast of Santa Ana—corn dance
September 29	Eve of Feast of San Geronimo— Sundown Dance
September 30	Feast of San Geronimo—trade fair, pole climbing ritual, foot races
December 24	Christmas Eve—Torchlight procession in honor of the Virgin, following vespers in the church
December 25	Matachines Dances and various animal dances in honor of the birth of Jesus

Clearly, the native heritage has melded harmoniously with the important days in the Christian calendar. The visitor to Taos Pueblo might take time during one of these events, or at any other time, to visit the Mission Church of San Geronimo which dates from 1847. The prior church was destroyed in the rebellion of the same year.

TAOS SKI VALLEY

The Taos Ski Valley is 19 miles northeast of the town of Taos via Highway 68 and then Highway 150 (also called the Ski Valley Road). There are: 71 trails with 24% beginner, 25% intermediate and 51% advanced; 7 chair and 2 poma lifts. Open daily during ski season from 9 a.m. to 4 p.m.; adult and child equipment rental services from $7 to $17 daily; snowmaking equipment; and on-slope lodging for about 1,200 skiers; many restaurants and bars. Out of the seemingly vast tangle of phone numbers, we have selected the following to help the visitor:

General Ski Valley Area information		505/776-2291
Same, but in downtown Taos		505/758-8283
Taos Ski Valley Snow Report		505/776-2916
Taos Valley Resort Association (reservation service)	800/992-7669	505/776-2233
Taos Central Reservations (Ski Valley and town of Taos)	800/821-2437	505/758-9767
Pride of Taos Shuttles (from airport and offers tours)		505/758-8340
Faust's Transportation	800/345-3738	505/758-3410/7359
Sleigh rides (operated by the Taos Pueblo)		505/758-3212

For a few more facts and figures: annual snowfall in the Ski Valley is about 325 inches, the elevations range from 9,207 feet to 11,819 feet with a vertical drop of 2,612 feet. There is a ski school (ranked No. 1 in the U.S. in Ski Magazine—October 1988), first-time learner programs and excellent emergency services. There are Taos-by-Night van-tour services operated by Pride of Taos Shuttles and Faust's for the skier to enjoy shopping, dining and culture in the town.

The lodges on the ski slopes offer meals and ski packages (lessons and lift tickets) at varying price ranges. *Austing Haus Hotel* (505/776-2649), *Hondo Lodge* (505/776-2277), *Hotel Edelweiss* (505/776-2301), *Hotel St. Bernard* (505/776-2251), *Innsbruck Lodge* (505/776-2313) and *Thunderbird Lodge* (505/776-2280) offer excellent rooms and meals. For those who desire housekeeping units on or near the ski slopes, *Kandahar Condos* (505/776-2226), *Rio Hondo Condos* (505/776-2646), *Sierra Del Sol Condos* (505/776-2981), *St. Bernard Condos* (505/776-8506) and *Twining Condos* (505/776-8648) offer modern, well-equipped rentals. Of course, there is the option to stay in town and drive into the Ski Valley (see our WHERE TO STAY section).

In the Taos Ski Valley, the *Boot Doctor* offers expert service in fitting ski boots and also in providing the correct skis and outfits (505/776-2489). The *Taos Ski Valley Sportswear, Ski and Rental Shops* (505/776-2291), located in the base area, provides ski equipment rental and sales, a store for apparel and full repair services for visitors. *Terry Sports* (800/821-2437 or in New Mexico 505/758-8522) has two centers, one in the Ski Valley and one in town on Paseo del Pueblo Norte for ski rentals, sales and service. To buy or rent ski equipment, try *Cottam's Ski Shops* with three locations in town and one in the Ski Valley (800/322-TAOS or in New Mexico 505/776-8540). In the town of Taos, there are two shops offering purchase and rental of ski equipment. *Olympic Ski Shops* (800/443-1321 or in New Mexico 505/776-1167) is a good bet. Also, *Sierra Sports* (505/758-2822) has budget rentals and good service. Many of the lodges offer elegant imported and domestic ski wear and after-ski wear.

Transportation is readily available from town or airport to the Ski Valley by public services. *Faust's Transportation* (800/345-3738, or in New Mexico 505/758-3410/758-7359) has daily local town-to-Ski Valley shuttle service in addition to its various airport routes. *Pride of Taos* (505/758-8340) operates shuttles from town to slopes with coordinated service for all Mesa Airline flights. Latest shuttle schedules are available by phone. For those in private cars, Ski Valley roads are meticulously maintained and well-sanded all winter.

The Taos Ski Valley was founded by the late Ernie Blake in 1955. There is perhaps no ski facility as spectacular and enchanting as this, his legacy. Also, a ski vacation here can be greatly enhanced with one of the most interesting and unique discovery vacations; the arts, nature, pueblo life, regional dining, incomparable subjects for photography, day trips and more are waiting for the tourist to sample. In the Taos Ski Valley itself, lofty peaks and sweeping views complement the powder snow and sun-filled days with skiing for every level of competence from beginner to Olympic status. According to California Magazine, " . . . Taos is one of the most interesting ski areas in the world, let alone in the Rocky Mountains." We endorse this opinion.

RANCHOS DE TAOS

Ranchos de Taos is located about four miles south of the Taos Plaza on South Santa Fe Road. This famous adobe church of San Francisco de Asís (St. Francis of Assisi) is the central point of interest. It has been the subject of painting and photography by many of the famous New Mexico artists. In fact, an entire book with 79 plates is devoted to just this subject (*Spirit and Vision: Images of Ranchos de Taos Church* by Sandra D'Emilio, Museum of New Mexico Press, 1987).

The most comfortable way to enjoy a visit to Ranchos de Taos and the church is to park in the ample space just east of the main road; here you will be directly behind the church. When General De Vargas returned to New Mexico, after the Pueblo Revolt, the Spanish settlers with him built a fort at Ranchos de Taos. After they had secured a safe place to live, trade and agriculture began to flourish. Unreliable legends have it that these settlers, under the guidance of the missionary fathers, started construction of a church; various dates are given as 1710, 1718, 1732-33. The adobe building you see today was probably built between 1812 and 1818; it is a splendid example of the European style of the Franciscans but fashioned out of local materials.

There are several shops for souvenirs, gifts and serious art in the area west (behind) the church. *Ranchos Ritz* (505/758-2640) features the work of nationally known artists along with fine jewelry and ceramics. *Celebrations* (505/758-1443) has not only reasonably priced presents, but also some fine artifacts. *R.B. Ravens* (505/758-1523) sells museum-grade art and ethnographic artifacts from the Southwest. Several other shops are worth browsing for souvenirs and collectibles. Connoisseur Jacqueline de Lusignan has opened *Hacienda de San Francisco Galeria* (505/758-0477) with some of the finest antique Spanish, Mexican and New Mexican furniture, arts and decorative items to be found in the state. A "must" for the serious collector.

A supper can be had at *Andy's Fiesta* which is located in one of the old fort buildings; steaks, seafood and northern New Mexican dishes are menu offerings along with full bar service. This interesting restaurant is open from 5:30 to 10 p.m., Tuesday through Saturday night. Best to call ahead for your reservation (505/758-9733). Another dining choice, *Don Pablo Gomez* (505/758-9281), Paseo del Pueblo Sur/South Santa Fe Road, serves Mexican and American cuisine for both luncheon and dinner. Open every day but Monday, wines and beers are served in this friendly restaurant. Mastercard and Visa are welcome. *Treats & Sweets & Something More* (505/758-1990) is a snack and candy shop in the parking lot area.

Camera buffs will have a fiesta of their own snapping all angles of the old church and the adobe buildings of the era. Across the street from the church is a U.S. Post Office for easy mailing of postcards and gifts to people back home. Two bed-and-breakfast inns are in the area: *Two Pipe* (505/758-4770) on the Talpa Route, Ranchos de Taos, NM 87557, a charming 275-year-old hacienda with a hot tub set in spacious gardens—rates start at $50; and *Whistling Waters* (505/758-7798) also on the Talpa Route, Ranchos de Taos, NM 87557. The rates start at $40 for a quiet stay in an old adobe house with cottonwoods in the courtyard.

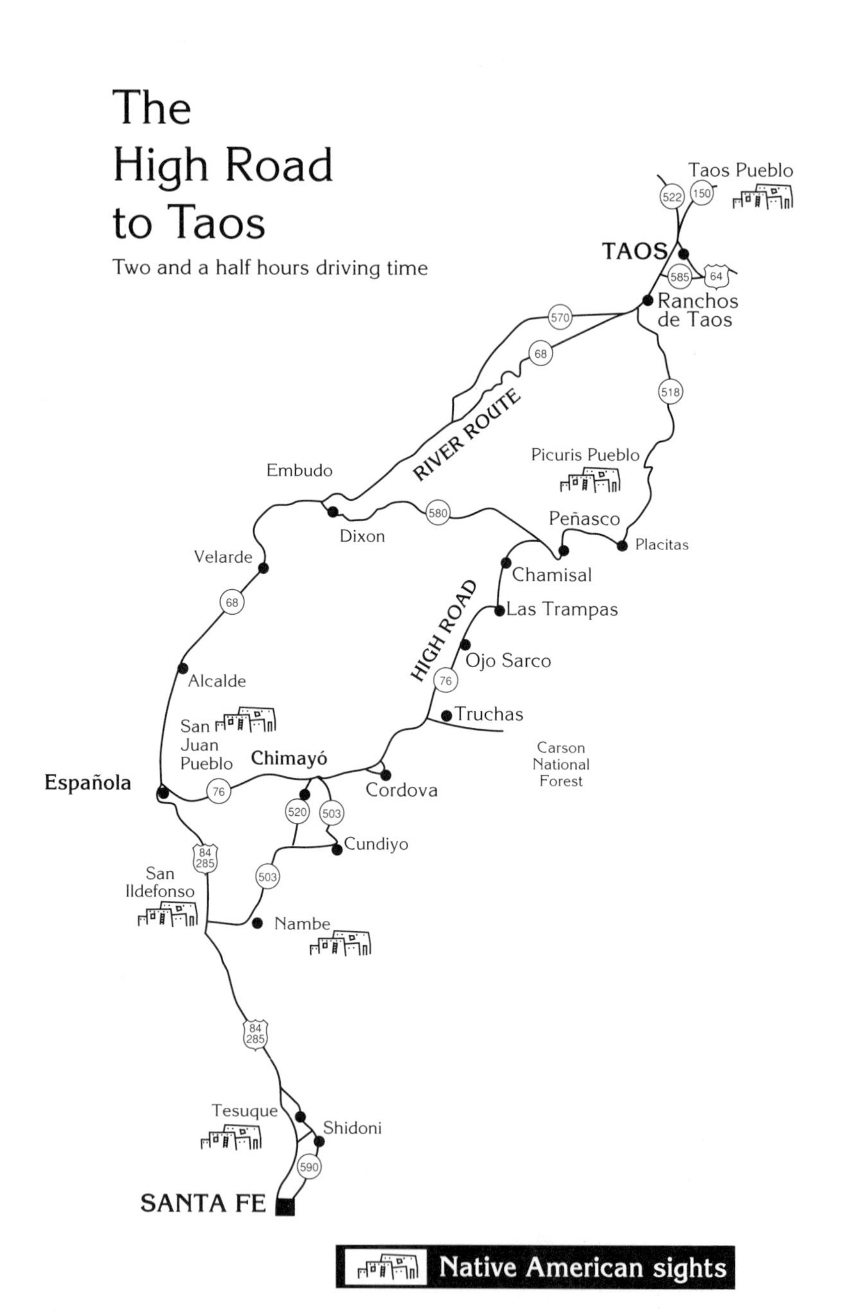
The
High Road
to Taos
Two and a half hours driving time
Taos Pueblo
522
150
TAOS
585
64
Ranchos
de Taos
570
68
518
RIVER ROUTE
Picuris Pueblo
Embudo
Dixon
580
Peñasco
Placitas
Velarde
Chamisal
HIGH ROAD
Las Trampas
68
Ojo Sarco
Alcalde
76
Truchas
San
Juan
Pueblo
Chimayó
Carson
National
Forest
Española
76
Cordova
520
503
Cundiyo
84
285
San
Ildefonso
503
Nambe
84
285
Tesuque
Shidoni
590
SANTA FE
Native American sights

TAKING THE HIGH ROAD TO TAOS

There's a hard choice to be made if you're planning to make a day trip from Santa Fe to Taos. Some folks will advise you to drive up on U.S. 285 and 68 and come back the same day on the High Road (Routes 518, 75 and 76).

That's fine, if you don't intend to spend much time in Taos, but there's quite a lot up there to see. The Taos Pueblo is one of the last of the multistory adobe pueblos, and you'll want to spend at least 30 or 40 minutes there. You'll find some good shops and galleries in Taos (we especially like Clay and Fibre). The Millicent Rogers Museum displays outstanding Indian antiques, and it houses a fully furnished *morada* (a Penitente chapel like those found in the northern villages), complete with a death cart. You should plan on spending an hour, perhaps more, seeing this excellent collection.

We think it's far better to make a full day of the trip to Taos (on U.S. 285 and N.M. 68) with a stop on the way. Then on another day, follow the High Road north from Santa Fe as far north as Las Trampas or, perhaps, Picuris Pueblo. Both drives are wonderful, and you won't want to be hurried.

However, if I had time for only one and not the other, I'd opt for the High Road, even though Aunt Tillie will say, "What? You didn't go to Taos?" The Spanish villages, the crafts and the countryside you'll see are, to me, unforgettable. They are the true essence of northern New Mexico. Tell Aunt Tillie that.

Going north on your Taos day trip, the one essential stop is the fruit-growing village of Velarde for a visit with Loretta Valdez. She and the ladies of the village fashion wreaths, ristras and other works of art from chiles, pine cones, seed pods, native grasses and other natural materials. You'll find Loretta at the Herman Valdez Fruit Stand on the west side of the highway at the north end of Velarde. Velarde is roughly halfway to Taos on N.M. 68.

The High Road trip begins north of Santa Fe when you turn off U.S. 285 in Pojoaque and take Route 503. Continue north and bear right to Cundiyo, a charming Spanish hillside village where almost everyone's surname is Vigil. Take note of the village church, with its sheet-metal cupola. There the village celebrates Christmas with old traditional songs and pageantry.

At the intersection with N.M. 76 turn east, and drive about a mile to a road on the right that drops down to the woodcarvers' village of Cordova. This is where santos, birds, animals and elaborate religious carvings are fashioned from cottonwood and cedar. George Lopez, the dean of carvers, lives in the first house on the right. He and the other craftspeople of Cordova show and sell their work in their homes. They welcome travelers.

From Cordova return to N.M. 76 and continue uphill and east to Truchas, a remote mountain village backed by the rugged Truchas Peaks. In the middle of the village watch for the turn to Las Trampas. The Las Trampas church, built about 1763, is considered a masterpiece of Spanish Colonial architecture. The village was once an adobe-walled town, and its vintage homes are reminiscent of 17th century Spanish houses.

From here, either go on to Picuris Pueblo to look around, or turn back, through Truchas, and head downhill for the weaving village of Chimayo, about two miles beyond the Cordova road. At the junction of N.M. 76 and 520 is Ortega's Weaving Shop, where several generations of the Ortega family can be seen at huge hand looms weaving traditional Spanish Colonial patterns into woolen rugs, jackets, vests and hangings that are sold in their large shop.

Less than a mile southeast on Route 520 is Rancho de Chimayó, the superb restaurant and guesthouse where members of the Jaramillo family are your hosts. Plan to stop there for lunch or dinner, and be sure to make reservations ahead (984-2100). Most of the menu is devoted to northern New Mexico specialties, and the *sopaipillas* are perhaps the best you'll find anywhere. In warm weather sit out on the terrace under the cottonwoods. In winter there is a big shepherd's fireplace to keep you warm.

A few hundred yards beyond the Rancho, on the other side of the river, is a dirt road branching off to the north. A small sign says Santuario de Chimayó. This beautiful twin-towered little church is built over a dry well, the dirt from which is said to have healed countless pilgrims. Believers walk there from all over the state on Good Friday. The well is in a room to the left of the altar, where some of those healed have left crutches, canes, santos and tributes. Since the church closes at dusk, you might want to visit here before you dine at the Rancho.

From Chimayó return to Santa Fe via Routes 520 (south), 503 (west) and U.S. 84-285 as you began.

Taos Pueblo Cemetary.

THE PUEBLOS

Legends, History, Dances, Feast Days, Directions

New Mexico, called the "Land of Enchantment," has many cultural treasures for the visitor to enjoy. None is more interesting than the pueblos, each with its unique features. Though there are similarities in the pueblos, it is the differences that make a visit to each pueblo a memorable experience.

Crafts from the hands of the resident artisans are for sale at nearly every pueblo. (However, in a few cases, some of the goods for sale are not made by the residents. It is best to examine labels and ask questions before making a purchase.)

There are three major Native American language families, and at least three variations of one of them, represented in the 19 pueblos. Some pueblos are tiny and some have vast land. Visitors should try to include several pueblos in their travel plans in order to reach a wider understanding of these Native Americans.

"Pueblo" means people, or village-where-the-people-live, and is the Spanish word meaning village. The Pueblo peoples primarily are cultural descendants of two Southwestern prehistoric cultures, the Anasazi (the Ancient Ones) and the Mogollon, and to a lesser extent the Sinagua, Salado and Hohokam peoples. By 700 A.D., the Anasazi had settled in Chaco Canyon, Puye Cliffs, Bandelier, the Jemez and other nearby locales. When the Spaniards arrived in 1539-40, they found many of the pueblos established, agrarian, theocratic communities, with housing made up of large multi-storied apartment or townhouse-like structures.

Many of those 80 pueblos have now vanished, but there are 19 pueblos still carrying on their historic traditions.

Internally, almost every pueblo society is divided into moieties, or summer and winter factions. These groups rule in seasonal rotations. However, San Ildefonso Pueblo is an exception to this pattern; its residents are called

North and South peoples. Pueblos are self-governing; they elect a governor and other officials who tend to both secular and sacred matters.

Basically, all pueblo ceremonies are religious in tradition and expression. As such, they deserve respectful conduct from all visitors. They are not mere fairs or bazaars. Most pueblos ask that visitors observe simple rules of etiquette: no drinking of alcohol, no photography or sketching (except by special permit), no recording and no entry into the sacred kivas. One does not shout or applaud the dancers, because Native American dances are sacred rituals, danced prayers. If you are lucky enough to be invited into a pueblo house, do be sure to taste the foods that will certainly be offered as a gesture of hospitality. To refuse would be considered rude. These foods are often prepared (for days ahead) by the host family in preparation for the great feast at hand.

The Christian celebrations are fixed by the calendar of the Catholic Church, while the Native American festivities are tied to the seasons; thus the dates will vary slightly from year to year. It is essential to check the exact dates, hours, and type of dance ceremony you plan to attend. Some dances and ceremonies are closed to outsiders. Call the pueblo to avoid disappointment.

The ceremonies stem from a complex set of symbols underlying all pueblo religious practices, as do the relationships of the residents to their many deities, their sacred lands, even to each other. There is considerable secrecy, or privacy, about the hidden aspects of all pueblo rituals.

Kachina, a Hopi word meaning spirit father, or father of life, is a supernatural being, a being who sends gifts and trials to humans and establishes laws on earth. But, at the popular level, a Kachina is a human who impersonates these supernatural forces at ceremonials. To the living, Kachinas can represent the departed ones. The Kachina dolls that tourists and collectors purchase depict these impersonators, and they correctly can be called *tihus*, or figures. Such a doll is a marvelous souvenir of New Mexico.

Some pueblos charge entry fees, and all have schedules of fees for photography, sketching, and painting. Camping and fishing fees are charged where such facilities are available.

In this directory, all area and population figures are necessarily approximate.

English and Spanish are spoken by many of the residents of the pueblos, and visitors will be welcomed when the pueblo is open to visitors. Again, always call ahead to verify the dates of dances and ceremonies.

Note: Photography, sketching, tape recording, note taking, etc. are strictly prohibited at ceremonial dances, unless permission is first obtained from tribal or pueblo officials. There is usually a fee involved and your receipt may be as simple as a piece of colored yarn.

The Old Church at Picuris Pueblo under reconstruction.

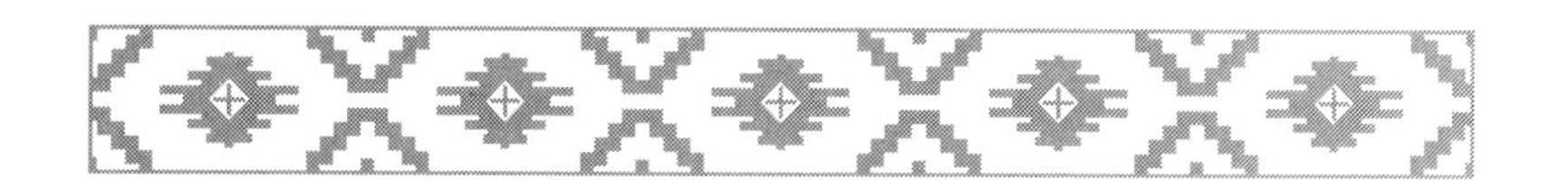

PUEBLOS OF NEW MEXICO

Acoma Pueblo

P.O. Box 309
Acomita, New Mexico 87043
505/552-6606

249,335 acres; population 2,268

Driving directions: *Take Interstate 40 west from Albuquerque, then take N.M. 23 from Paraje south about 13 miles to the pueblo.*

Important data: Admission fee (discount for senior citizens). Visitors' center from which guided tours start. Photography fee. Picnics for a fee at the pueblo. Fishing permits for Acomita Lake and the San Jose River are issued for a fee; fishing season March 15-October 31. Camping and RV park at nearby Gallup (38 miles west). Picnickers welcome.

The Acoma Pueblo Museum contains exhibits of native pottery dating from 1400 A.D.

Acoma is a Registered National Historic Landmark.

Note: The pueblo is closed to the public in mid-July and early October.

Feast day: September 2. On this day, the pueblo honors San Esteban (St. Stephen of Hungary).

Language: Keresan

Mission church: San Esteban del Rey (founded in 1629). Except for a hiatus during the Pueblo Revolt period (1680-1692), the mission church of San Esteban del Rey has been in continuous use since its founding.

Acoma Pueblo is set on a massive sandstone rock mesa (a *penol*) about 50 miles west of Albuquerque. The central village of the pueblo is known as "The Sky City" because of its 400-foot elevation above a great plateau.

Acoma is certainly one of the oldest pueblos, established about 900 A.D. Inhabitants have been there continuously since 1075 A.D. and, anthropologists say, in the area since 3000 B.C.

On the way into the pueblo proper, you pass the famous Enchanted Mesa. This awesome rock formation stands alone in a dramatic setting which the Puebloans are said to have used for religious rites and secret pilgrimages. The Indians call the great rock Katsim, and the Spanish name is Mesa Encantada. It is said that before time needed to be recorded, three Indian women became stranded out on the range far from the village. A violent storm came up and destroyed all rescue trails. During the cataclysm, the Enchanted Mesa was fashioned by the elements. One by one, the women perished atop the isolated mesa, and to this day the belief is that the spirits of the three women inhabit the Enchanted Mesa. Just beyond this spot is the Acoma Pueblo which is on yet another rock mesa.

Many Acoma men raise livestock and women fashion pottery. Acoma pottery is distinguished by its fine black geometric designs on a white slip. These pots are so finely crafted and fired that they are not only highly decorative but also watertight.

All visitors must park at the Information Center below the "Sky Mesa" to register, pay fees and board the official bus that takes them up to the Pueblo for a 45-minute tour.

Cochiti Pueblo

P.O. Box 70
Cochiti Pueblo, New Mexico 87040
505/465-2244

29,799.03 acres; population 613

Driving directions: *Take Interstate 25 (north out of Albuquerque or South out of Santa Fe) and then turn west on N.M. 22 for seven miles, then two more miles north* *on N.M. 16 to pueblo direction signs.*

Important data: No photography, recording or sketching permitted at any time. Fishing permits issued for a fee. Hunting permits (for dove and duck) issued for a fee. No picnics, camping or RV facilities.

Feast day: July 14. On this day, the pueblo honors San Buenaventura (St. Bonaventure).

Language: Keresan

Mission church: San Buenaventura. The original mission church was completed by the close of the 17th century; the present church was finished about 100 years later.

Present-day Cochiti Pueblo has been occupied since the 14th century A.D. The Cochiti people have a deep ancestral connection to the Anasazi of the Chaco Canyon area.

Cochiti craftspeople enjoy great popularity. The famous "Storyteller" pottery designs created by Helen Cordero have won her international fame. Mrs. Cordero's pottery creations feature a mother figure with clusters of children huddled close together listening to tales from the clay storyteller. They are highly prized by collectors.

Great double-headed drums of aspen or cottonwood are made at this pueblo. Entire families devote themselves to the creation of drums from seasoned aspen or cottonwood logs hollowed with chisel and hammer. For many years, Cochiti drums have been sold and traded with the other pueblos, so the pueblo dance drums seen up and down the Rio Grande Valley are mostly from Cochiti (except at Taos, where the people make their own).

The peace the Cochiti farmer and artisan enjoyed for centuries was interrupted in 1975, when the U.S. Corps of Engineers built one of the nation's largest earth-filled flood control dams across the Rio Grande. The resulting lake does provide recreational boating and fishing, but farm fields and the ecology of the area have been harmed.

On the feast day, July 14, the two pueblo *moieties*, the Turquoise and the Squash, perform dances in front of the two kivas after morning mass.

Isleta Pueblo

P.O. Box 317
Isleta Pueblo, New Mexico 87002
505/869-3111

211,026.31 acres; population 2,289

Driving directions: *Take Interstate 25 south out of Albuquerque. Continue south on N.M. 85 directly into the pueblo. The total distance from Albuquerque is about 13 miles.*

Important data: No photography, recording or sketching is permitted at any time except for photos of the mission church. Fishing permits issued for a fee. No hunting available. Picnics, camping, and RV at the Pueblo's Isleta Lakes for a fee (505/877-0370). Isleta, within 15 miles of Albuquerque, offers Albuquerque's visitors an opportunity to see a pueblo with a fine, old church in less than a half-day's tour.

Feast day: August 28. On this day, the pueblo honors San Agustin (St. Augustine). *Note:* During the 1600s and up to 1710 the patron saint of Isleta was San Antonio.

Language: Tiwa (a variation of Tanoan)

Mission church: The mission church of San Agustin claims to be the oldest mission church in the state, with fragments of the wall and foundation dating to 1613. Isleta Pueblo is the largest of the Tiwa language group. The principal settlement is west of the Rio Grande just north of Los Lunas. The Isleta people have occupied their lands from a time that predates the Coronado expedition of 1540. Historically, the pueblo served as a stop for almost every overland expedition, explorer, or band of travelers that came upstream through the Rio Grande Valley. The Isleta peoples were the only Pueblo Indians who did not join the Pueblo Revolt of 1680. Instead, some members fled south to El Paso del Norte (now Ciudad Juarez); others went into Hopi territory (now part of Arizona). Most of them eventually returned to Isleta.

Isleta Pueblo history was made when a woman governor was elected in 1987.

Many Isletans are still involved with traditional arts, crafts and trades: agriculture, animal husbandry, making of bakery products, jewelry and embroidery. Some pueblo members commute daily to work in Albuquerque in private business or with the military.

Jemez Pueblo

P.O. Box 78
Jemez Pueblo, New Mexico 87024
505/834-7359

88,860.22 acres; population 1,504

Driving directions: *Take N.M. 44 west from Bernalillo to San Ysidro, then N.M. 4 north to the pueblo. Total distance from the Bernalillo exit on Interstate 25 is about 30 miles.*

Important data: No photography, recording or sketching is permitted at any time. Fishing and game hunting permits are issued for a fee. No picnics, no camping or RV facilities.

Feast day: November 12. On this day, the pueblo honors San Diego (St. James).

Language: Towa (a variation of Tanoan). This is the last remaining pueblo to speak this language.

Mission church: San Diego de Alcala (St. James)

The famous dances at Jemez Pueblo are worth making an effort to go to see. Each year, early in August, there is a feast (*porcingula*) and dancing in honor of Our Lady of the Angels, who was the patron of the Pecos Pueblo.

Pecos Pueblo, ravaged by disease and attacked by Plains Indians, was abandoned by 17 survivors who were welcomed by the Jemez Pueblo in 1838. Now the celebration day features spectacular dances (including the Pecos Bull dance), food stalls, music, and clowns, and attracts many spectators.

On December 12, the traditional feast day for Our Lady of Guadalupe, there is a mass, followed by communal eating in a tent in the open plaza of the pueblo. This is the day the Mexican-style Matachines dance is performed (alternating with an Indian-style Matachines group) featuring the traditional maiden, *malinche*, and some very fancy footwork. The Matachines dance has roots in Mexico and earlier, in Moorish Spain. The Mexican-style troupe wear masked headdresses with long streamers and lace leggings over their trousers. The dancers move to the music of a fiddler and dry gourd rattles. This celebration has gone on at Jemez for more than 40 years.

Woven belts, yucca fiber baskets, and cloth for garments are the primary crafts of Jemez Pueblo. In addition, the Pecos Pueblo descendants have revived pottery making. They use clay found near Pecos Pueblo, and decorate the vessels with traditional glazes.

Jemez is known and admired for its daring Hot Shots, a company of forest fire fighters who are called to all parts of the United States to quell out-of-control forest blazes.

Laguna Pueblo

P.O. Box 194
Laguna Pueblo, New Mexico 87026
505/243-7616 or 552-6651

440,940.74 acres; population 3,564

Driving directions: *Take Interstate 40 west from Albuquerque about 40 miles. Portions of the pueblo are on the highway, but to drive deeper into the Pueblo, take N.M. 279 north.*

Important data: Photography permits issued for a fee. Fishing permits issued for a fee (there is a large reservoir at the pueblo). No picnics, camping or RV facilities.

Feast day: September 19. On this day, the pueblo honors San Jose (St. Joseph). There is a great fair to which Indians from all over New Mexico come to trade or sell crafts and produce. Another feast day, March 19, also honors San Jose.

Language: Keresan

Mission church: San Jose de Laguna (St. Joseph). Construction of the mission church was begun by the end of the 17th century and finished by 1706.

Laguna is a pueblo that is both very modern and very traditional. Under the lands held by Laguna Pueblo are some of the richest uranium deposits in the world. There are also reserves of top quality marble. Lagunans tend their livestock much as their ancestors did.

The pueblo and the mission of San Jose date from 1699.

The Laguna land reaches to the foot of Mt. Taylor. Driving through the reservation, one passes fruit trees, corrals and farmland, and may savor the aroma of baking bread from the beehive-shaped outdoor adobe ovens, called *hornos*.

Laguna Pueblo is often referred to as the Laguna Pueblos because there are six satellite villages in addition to Laguna proper. The villages are Casa Blanca, Encinal, Mesita, Paguate, Paraje and Seama. In turn, Seama has three mini-suburban residential areas called Harrisburg, New York and Philadelphia.

The principal settlement of Laguna Pueblo is readily visible from Interstate 40. The most prominent structure, set above clusters of low adobe buildings, is the whitewashed adobe mission church of San Jose de Laguna. Within the historic church the altar screen and the old leather canopy, with a tableau of the heavens (sun, moon, stars and rainbow), are unspoiled examples of early New Mexican sacred art.

Nambe Pueblo

Route 1, Box 177-BB
Santa Fe, New Mexico 87501
505/455-7692 or 455-7752

19,075.99 acres; population 175

Driving directions: *Take U.S. 84/285 north out of Santa Fe about 16 miles to the Nambe River Bridge in Pojoaque, turn east on N.M. 4 and drive about five miles (through Nambe) to pueblo direction signs, turn east and drive another two miles to the pueblo.*

Important data: Photography permits issued for a fee. Fishing, boating and picnic permits issued for a fee. No hunting available. Picnics, camping and RV facilities available at Nambe Lake (run by the pueblo) (505) 455-2304.

Feast day: October 4. On this day, the pueblo honors San Francisco de Asis (St. Francis of Assisi).

Language: Tewa (a variation of Tanoan)

Mission Church: San Francisco de Assisi

Nambe Pueblo, a short drive from Santa Fe, is at the foot of the spectacular Sangre de Cristo mountains. The pueblo proper is now encircled by non-pueblo housing. Although many Nambe Pueblo residents have been absorbed into the general work force of the local area, there is a keen interest in ancestral traditions. Weaving and pottery are principal crafts, and traditional dancing keeps the past alive.

Near the pueblo, at Nambe Falls, there is an annual, spirited July 4th celebration. However, the principal feast with traditional dancing is held on October 4, the feast day of St. Francis, the pueblo patron saint. There are other dances held during the year, including Kings' Day on the Sunday nearest January 6. These dances take place in the plaza near the pueblo kiva.

Picuris Pueblo

P.O. Box 228
Peñasco, New Mexico 87533
505/587-2519

14,946.88 acres; population 116

Driving directions: *Take N.M. 68 north out of Española, turn east on N.M. 75 (through Dixon). Turn north into the pueblo at the markers (which are easy to miss) as you approach Peñasco.*

Important data: Photography permits issued for a fee. Fishing permits issued for a fee, year-round. No hunting available. Archeological ruins are open to the public. No picnic, camping or RV facilities available.

Feast day: August 10. On this day, the pueblo honors San Lorenzo (St. Lawrence).

Language: Tiwa (a variation of Tanoan)

Mission church: San Lorenzo (Picuris Pueblo is sometimes called San Lorenzo Pueblo). A wall near this church is built of puddled adobe, and is one of very few remaining structures using this pre-Spanish building method, where mud is laid directly on the wall in courses and allowed to dry. Adobe bricks were not used in the region until introduced by the Spanish. In 1776, the mission of San Lorenzo de Picuris was in the process of being rebuilt on an older foundation.

The ancestors of Picuris Pueblo (together with those Indians who eventually settled Taos) probably came into the area about 900 A.D. The first pueblo (now an archeological ruin close to the present-day settlement) dates from about 1150 A.D. From early times, the Picuris people had contact with the Plains tribes, and this cross-cultural exchange is evident in Picuris' ceremonial practices and dress styles. The residents here were deeply involved with the Pueblo Revolt of 1680 against the Spanish.

Picuris Pueblo has a community building that houses not only a crafts training center with a gallery shop but also a small museum with tribal treasures. Some of the women fashion pottery from sparkling micaceous clay.

In June, 1985 the pueblo sponsored its first outdoor summer arts fair. A variety of crafts and native foods is offered for sale to the public at this colorful event.

Pojoaque Pueblo

(pronounced "Po-WALK-ee")
Rt. 1, Box 71
Santa Fe, New Mexico 87501
505/455-2278

11,602.37 acres; population 94

Driving directions: *The pueblo is on U.S. 84/285 north of Santa Fe about 16 miles. The visitor is urged to stop at the Pojoaque tourist center for guidance.*

Important data: Photography permits issued for a fee. No fishing or hunting available. There is a newly established tourist information center on U.S. 84/285 (telephone 505/455-3460). Picnic, camping and RV facilities are available on the highway lands of the pueblo (not inside the village area).

Feast day: December 12. On this day, the pueblo honors the Virgin of Guadalupe.

Language: Tewa (a variation of Tanoan)

Parish church: Nuestra Señora de Guadalupe de Pojoaque (Our Lady of Guadalupe Church of Pojoaque)

The pueblo at Pojoaque has no delineated village center. The present pueblo area has been inhabited since about 1300 A.D.; a 1598 map shows that the Pojoaque region was inhabited then. In the 19th century, Pojoaque dwindled to 40 residents. From 1912 to 1932, the pueblo was temporarily abandoned due to epidemics.

Pojoaque Pueblo has since inaugurated vigorous enterprises. The pueblo land along the highway and in Pojoaque Plaza has been leased to many businesses and shops. There is a pueblo-operated camping area. Industrial activities include both mica and pumice works. There are also the traditional crafts of pottery, beading and jewelry. Pojoaque was the first modern pueblo to elect a woman governor, who held office from 1973 to 1974.

Our Lady of Guadalupe is venerated on December 12 with special pueblo activities. After mass at the parish church, there is traditional dancing and feasting in pueblo homes. The public is invited to attend these events. In 1986 the Butterfly dance was performed at Pojoaque for the first time in over 50 years.

San Ildefonso Pueblo

Route 5, Box 315-A
Santa Fe, New Mexico 87501
505/455-2273

460,401.99 acres; population 488

Driving directions: *Take U.S. 84/285 north out of Santa Fe, then N.M. 4 northwest (the Los Alamos road) about seven miles. Pueblo signs mark the entrance.*

Important data: Photography and fishing permits issued for a fee. No hunting available. No picnics, camping or RV facilities.

Feast day: January 23. On this day, the pueblo honors St. Ildefonse who was an archbishop of Toledo, Spain, in the 7th century.

Language: Tewa (a variation of Tanoan)

Mission church: San Ildefonso. The early mission church, which stood from the beginning of the 18th century, has been copied in the new structure dedicated in 1968.

San Ildefonso Pueblo is said to have been established by 1300 A.D. Today, it is known for its outgoing and hospitable people and for their world-famous black-on-black pottery.

In the 1920s, there was a rift among the pueblo residents that resulted in two religious and family factions. One group stayed on the north side of the pueblo (in the direction of the sacred Black Mesa), and the other group remained close to the round kiva, still very prominent in the pueblo plaza. These moieties, factions or groups, are uniquely called the North and the South people. Today, the split has healed but the North and South designation remains.

Many of the pueblo residents now work in Los Alamos. However, there are also the traditional occupations of farming and pottery making. The late Maria Martinez achieved international distinction for her artistry as a potter of the black-on-black designs.

One of the most interesting and spectacular ceremonial events in New Mexico is the feast of San Ildefonso on January 23. The pre-dawn ritual drama is memorable. Visitors begin to arrive at the pueblo by 5 a.m. to await the pueblo men, dressed in authentic animal-hide costumes (such as deer, coyote, etc.) who appear at the horizon. These eerie creatures silently move over the hills into the pueblo center. After this ancient, traditional dramatization, there is a mass at the pueblo mission church. Throughout the day, there is a dance program; the Comanche-style dancers in one plaza alternate with animal dance groups in the other.

For those visiting New Mexico in winter, the ceremony can be an unforgettable experience quite in contrast with skiing and souvenir shopping. Photography of limited subjects is permitted, for fees usually under five dollars. Extra warm clothing is a must, and a thermos of hot soup or coffee is recommended.

Because this ceremony is essentially religious, visitors are not always permitted to watch the early-morning gathering.

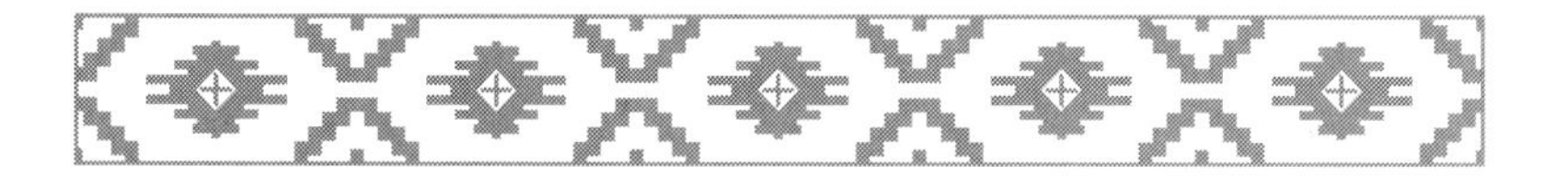

San Juan Pueblo

P.O. Box 1099
San Juan Pueblo, New Mexico 87566
505/852-4400

12,234.23 acres; population 852

Driving directions: *Take U.S. 84/285 north from Santa Fe (both highways 84 and 285 will turn west in Española. do not take either). Continue north through Española on N.M. 68. Turn west on N.M. 74 and continue one mile into the pueblo.*

Important data: Photography permits issued for a fee. Fishing and small game hunting permits issued for a fee. Picnics can be held at the tribal lake. No camping or RV facilities available.

San Juan Pueblo is host to the Eight Northern Indian Pueblo Council. It is also home to the Oke Oweenge Arts and Crafts Cooperative.

There is a modern bed-and-breakfast facility, Chinguagua Compound (P.O. Box 1118, San Juan Pueblo 87566, 505/852-2194).

Feast day: June 24. On this day, the pueblo honors San Juan (St. John the Baptist).

Language: Tewa (a variation of Tanoan)

Parish church: San Juan Bautista

In 1598, the Spaniards under Oñate established their first capital in the kingdom of New Mexico at San Juan (then located on the west side of the river). A brief period of harmony gave way to Indian hatred of Spanish domination. San Juan was the home of Popé, a medicine man, who became the leader of the bloody Pueblo Revolt of 1680. He was a pueblo patriot dedicated to forcing the Spaniards off all Indian lands. In time, he became a tyrant and some of his people lost faith in him, thus weakening their cause. By 1692-1693, the Spaniards under De Vargas were once again the rulers of *Nuevo México*.

San Juan Pueblo has assumed a place of leadership among the northern pueblos becaue of its vigor in promoting Tiwa and Tewa ventures. San Juan is active in the production of traditional crafts, especially red or brown pottery. Many of the men are expert woodcarvers. Those products and fine jewelry are for sale in the Oke Oweenge Crafts Cooperative.

Sandia Pueblo

P.O. Box 608
Bernalillo, New Mexico 87004
505/867-3317

22,884.45 acres; population 217

Driving directions: *Sandia is about 14 miles north of Albuquerque on US 85. From the center of Bernalillo take U.S. 85 south for about three miles. Turn east into the pueblo at the marker.*

Important data: No photography or recording are permitted at any time. No fishing or hunting available. No picnic, camping or RV facilities.

Feast day: June 13. On this day, the pueblo honors San Antonio de Padua (St. Anthony of Padua).

Language: Tiwa (a variation of Tanoan)

Mission church: San Antonio de Padua

"Sandia" means watermelon in Spanish. At sunset, the Sandia Mountains, which rise from the eastern part of the pueblo lands, turn to the color of the interior of a watermelon.

By 1300 A.D., there were inhabitants at Sandia Pueblo. During Coronado's encampment in the area (at the now extinct Mohi Pueblo) from 1540 to 1541, the Spanish leader certainly visited Sandia. The mission of San Francisco was leveled during the Pueblo Revolt of 1680, and residents fled west into Hopi territory for safety. History records that a kindly padre, Fr. Delgado, led the Sandia people back to their lands by 1748. In the 1890s, the present-day mission was built.

Sandia is a very conservative pueblo, and its ceremonies are still held in deep secrecy.

Sandia's location on the rim of the state's largest city, Albuquerque, has forced changes on the settlement but has also provided new jobs for its residents. A principal source of income for the pueblo is rental fees charged the operators of the Sandia Crest tramway. This tramway takes visitors, hikers and skiers to the summit of the mountains and operates all year. Also, the Sandia pueblo farmers have opened a new "U-pick-it-yourself" produce farm which is open to the public during the growing season.

San Felipe Pueblo

P.O. Box 308
Algodones, New Mexico 87001
505/867-3381, 867-3382 and 867-3383

48,852.76 acres; population 1,789

Driving directions: *There are two San Felipe highway direction signs on Interstate 25 about halfway between Albuquerque and Santa Fe. Turn west at either and drive directly into the pueblo.*

Important data: No photography, recording or sketching permitted at any time. No fishing or hunting available. No picnic, camping or RV facilities.

Feast day: May 1. On this day, the pueblo honors San Felipe (St. Philip).

Language: Keresan

Mission church: The mission church of San Felipe was first constructed in 1706 and records indicate the present church was reconstructed by 1736. The old retablo is of the period.

San Felipe Pueblo is still one of the more conservative pueblos in the state of New Mexico. It has earned a well-deserved reputation for some of the most remarkable ceremonial events of any pueblo. The two most outstanding ceremonies are those on Christmas Eve and at the Feast of St. Philip on May 1. The Christmas Eve services are held in the mission church, and the public is invited to attend. The traditional manger tableau, the mass and the altar with Christmas greens are all evidence of a Christian ceremony. But the music of drums and young boys blowing wooden whistles, together with pre-Christian Indian dances, make this a stunning ecumenical event. Then in the spring, the same blend of Christian and the traditional Indian rituals takes place for the Corn Dance and fiesta to honor San Felipe, the pueblo patron. Hundreds of dancers, male and female, perform in the large, concave central plaza.

The pueblo was most probably inhabited by the 1500s, and farming was the traditional occupation along with crafts that supplied the people's needs. Today, some farming is still done but crafts have all but vanished. Most residents work outside of the pueblo.

Santa Ana Pueblo

P.O. Box 37
Bernalillo, New Mexico 87004
505/867-3301

44,618.26 acres; population 407

Driving directions: *From the Bernalillo exit on Interstate 25, take N.M. 44 west for about nine miles. Turn north into the pueblo at the marker.*

Important data: No photography, recording or sketching is permitted at any time. No hunting or fishing is available. No picnic, camping or RV facilities.

Feast day: July 26. On this day, the pueblo honors Santa Ana (St. Ann).

Language: Keresan

Mission church: Santa Ana. This church was finished by the middle of the 18th century and houses an original 19th century retablo.

Although archeological ruins of ceremonial chambers dating to about 1350 A.D. have been found at the Coronado State Monument near Santa Ana Pueblo, that site is not the foundation for the present pueblo. Santa Ana Pueblo has probably been occupied since the early 1500s; Coronado saw it in 1540.

Because of a shortage of water, many of the Santa Ana people live near Bernalillo in a settlement known as Ranchos de Santa Ana. The pueblo itself is semi-abandoned and closed to visitors except for ceremonial events. At that time the Santa Ana people return for feasting and dancing. Some few crafts are still produced in the old village including pottery, wood carving and the manufacture of hand-fashioned wooden crosses with straw inlay. These unique religious items are highly valued collectors' treasures.

Santa Clara Pueblo

P.O. Box 580
Espanola, New Mexico 87532
505/753-7326

45,744.18 acres; population 1,839

Driving directions: *Take U.S. 84/285 north from Santa Fe, then N.M. 4 west (towards Los Alamos) to N.M. 30. Go north for about eight miles to the markers.*

Important data: Photography permits issued for a fee. Fishing permits issued for a fee. Guided tour packages to Puye Cliff Dwellings, Tuesdays and Thursdays throughout the year. Picnics and camping permitted in Santa Clara Canyon but not at the pueblo.

Feast day: August 12. On this day, the pueblo honors Santa Clara (St. Clare).

Language: Tewa (a variation of Tanoan)

Mission church: Santa Clara. There is also a Baptist mission.

Puye Cliff Dwellings are a Registered National Historic Landmark.

Santa Clara Pueblo occupies the same site it did when the Spaniards arrived in the 1540s. There was most certainly a prior pueblo near this spot that could date to around 1300 A.D.; the pueblo was moved several times. The people of Santa Clara link their ancestors to the Puye Cliff dwellers, and even earlier, to those of the Pajarito Plateau. The first mission was established in 1620, and the present church dates from 1918. During the 1800s, the pueblo was afflicted with tribal disputes and epidemics. But since 1935, Santa Clara has been considered a progressive pueblo.

Most famous of the Santa Clara crafts is the polished black pottery. Fashioned into impressive vessels, the potter's craft is at its apex here.

Santa Clara Pueblo is also known locally as *Kapo.*

The Puye Cliff cave dwellings and ruin are most interesting and may be seen about four miles south of the pueblo. Outstanding picnic and campsites, among several lakes and a stream, are available just west of Puye in Santa Clara Canyon.

Santo Domingo Pueblo

General Delivery
Santo Domingo Pueblo, New Mexico 87052
505/465-2214

69,259.82 acres; population 2,139

Driving directions: *Turn off Interstate 25 (between Santa Fe and Albuquerque) onto N.M. 22. Go west about six miles and follow the markers into the pueblo.*

Important data: No photography, recording or sketching permitted at any time. No fishing or hunting available. No picnic, camping or RV facilities.

Feast day: August 4. On this day, the pueblo honors Santo Domingo (St. Dominic).

Language: Keresan

Mission church: Santo Domingo. The first mission church was demolished during the Pueblo Revolt of 1680; the church in place now is about 90 years old.

There are problems in dating the Santo Domingo Pueblo, due to the persistent flooding of the area by the Rio Grande. The Spanish visited the pueblo in 1592. During the Pueblo Revolt of 1680, the residents fled to the

Jemez Mountain region; within three years most had returned to the pueblo, only to flee again in 1692 with the arrival of De Vargas. The first mission church was built in 1605. The pueblo, a very conservative one, is known for its abiding traditions. In addition to producing stunning silver jewelry, the craftspeople of Santo Domingo make necklaces of heishi (tiny pieces of shell which are cut, drilled, strung, then rounded by grinding through sandstone troughs). The pottery is excellent, if not innovative. When the Santa Fe Railroad crossed the Southwest in 1880, trains would make a reservation stop here so that passengers could buy Indian wares. Santo Domingo artists now take their crafts to the Palace of the Governors and shops in Santa Fe and Albuquerque to sell them.

The ceremonial dances at Santo Domingo are magnificent. One of the most famous is the annual Green Corn Dance on August 4 to honor St. Dominic, the pueblo's patron. The winter and summer moieties, called Turquoise and Squash, dance throughout the day in a vast central plaza. It is another instance of the meshing of Catholic and pre-Christian ritual elements, and features great masses of colorful dancers of all ages.

Taos Pueblo

P.O. Box 1846
Taos Pueblo, New Mexico 87571
505/758-8626; 758-9593

95,330.91 acres; population 716

Driving directions: *Take N.M. 68 north from the town of Taos and follow the markers to the pueblo.*

Important data: There is an admission fee (discount for Senior Citizens in bus groups). Photography permits issued for a fee. No fishing or hunting available. No picnic, camping or RV facilities. (The town of Taos offers RV parks.) Taos Pueblo is a Registered National Historic Landmark.

Feast day: September 30. On this day, the pueblo honors San Geronimo (St. Jerome).

Language: Tiwa (a branch of Tanoan)

Mission church: San Geronimo

Taos Pueblo is the northernmost of the New Mexico pueblos and certainly the most photographed. Research indicates that the north building has been continuously occupied longer than any other residential structure in the United States. This adobe "apartment house" was built about 1450 A.D., and the south building somewhat later. These multistoried dwellings have fascinated historians, artists, photographers and anthropologists. Tradition and respect for the earth dictate that there be no piped water or electricity in the adobe structures. The stream running between them is the source of household water.

The pueblo has been the scene of many conflicts. It was long a trading center, drawing Indians, traders and trappers from all over the West to its markets. Taos has also been the stage for many spectacular dance performances each year. The land, set against a backdrop of New Mexico's highest mountain (Wheeler Peak: 13,161 feet), is suited to both agriculture and grazing. Taos residents who pursue traditional occupations manufacture jewelry, drums, quivers and carvings, the famous Taos moccasins and boots with thick hide soles and soft doeskin tops.

More details are to be found in the Taos section of this book.

Tesuque Pueblo

(pronounced "Tess-OO'-key")
Route 1, Box 1
Santa Fe, New Mexico 87501
505/983-2667

16,810.66 acres; population 235

Driving directions: *Take U.S. 84/285 north from Santa Fe. Just beyond the Santa Fe Opera, turn west at marker and continue just under one mile into the pueblo.*

Important data: Photography permits issued for a fee. No hunting or fishing available. Picnic and camping grounds at pueblo-operated Camel Rock Campground on U.S. 84/285.

Feast day: November 12. On this day, the pueblo honors San Diego (St. James).

Language: Tewa (a variation of Tanoan)

Mission church: San Diego

Tesuque Pueblo may have been established before 1300 A.D. It was here that the famous Pueblo Revolt of 1680 started and spread. The first mission church was destroyed during the hostilities. The residents of the pueblo, then a few miles west of the present-day center, went to join other rebellious Tewas near the Black Mesa.

The people of Tesuque Pueblo are engaged in traditional occupations. The men are involved with agriculture, and the women craft pottery. Most of their clay items are small figurines decorated with bright paint.

The Christmas Day dances are some of the most colorful to be held near Santa Fe. On that day, visitors may stop by for a few hours throughout the day to watch the celebrations in the central plaza of Tesuque Pueblo.

Zia Pueblo

General Delivery
San Ysidro, New Mexico 87053
505/867-3304

112,510.51 acres; population 524

Driving directions: *From the Bernalillo exit on Interstate 25, take N.M. 44 west for about 16 miles. Turn north into the pueblo at the marker.*

Important data: No photography, recording or sketching permitted at any time. No fishing or hunting available. No picnic, camping or RV facilities.

Feast day: August 15. On this day, the pueblo celebrates the feast of the Assumption of the Virgin Mary.

Language: Keresan

Mission church: Nuestra Señora de la Asunción (Our Lady of the Assumption) was established in 1694 and the church in place at present dates from a decade or so later.

Zia Pueblo has given a remarkable and permanent gift to New Mexico: the sun symbol, which is seen everywhere. The Zia sun symbol originated from a Zia Pueblo pottery design in which there were three rays on a side. In the present version, the four top rays are said to stand for the winds of the four directions, the rays on the right represent the divisions of the day into morning, noon, afternoon and night, the ones at the bottom for the four seasons, and those at the left represent the stages of infancy, childhood, adulthood, old age. Dr. H. P. Mera designed the state flag with this emblem in the center, and the legislature gave its official approval in 1925. The Zia design is not only the approved symbol of the state flag, it is also the official emblem used on the New Mexico license plates, and unofficially on all manner of tourist items, tiles, T-shirts and more. Another design of the Zia artisans is the rain-bird motif. The potters of the pueblo are skilled and produce pots of unglazed terra cotta with a white slip.

Pueblo peoples have lived near or on this site since about 1300 A.D. The Indians are said to have migrated from higher in the Jemez Mountains. Their present location gives the Zias direct access to the Jemez River.

Zuni Pueblo

P.O. Box 339
Zuni Pueblo, New Mexico 87327
505/782-4481

406,190.96 acres; population 5,988

Driving directions: *Take Interstate 40 west from Albuquerque to Gallup (about 140 miles). Turn south on N.M. 32 for about 30 miles, then west another eight miles into the pueblo.*

Important data: Photography permits issued for a fee. No fishing or hunting available. At Blackrock, which is three miles east of the pueblo, there is an RV camping area.

Feast day: There is no official pueblo feast day. The great Shalako celebration in late November or early December is the major annual religious event. However, on December 12 (feast for Our Lady of Guadalupe) and June 13 (feast of St. Anthony of Padua) there are special masses.

Language: Zunian

Mission church: St. Anthony's and the old (now restored) Mission of Our Lady of Guadalupe. There are also Baptist and Christian Reformed missions. The Catholic mission at Zuni has had a mercurial history. Built in 1629 but first dedicated to the Virgin of Guadalupe in 1699, it has had several dedications following destructions of the structure. By 1754, the mission was permanently placed under the spiritual name of Guadalupe. The present church is a 1969 reconstruction.

Zuni is the largest of the Indian Pueblos and the first to have been seen by the Spaniards under Coronado in July, 1540. It was six large cities then. Coronado thought he had found Cibola, until he noticed that the streets weren't paved with gold.

Perhaps the most widely known of all the Indian ceremonials in New Mexico is the annual Shalako ceremony which takes place in late November or early December at Zuni Pueblo. It is important to understand that the word Shalako has three separate meanings: the annual ceremonial dance ritual, an artistic image in the form of a living impersonation of a carved figure, and an Indian spiritual concept.

The stunning Shalako ceremony is a year in the planning and includes roles for such characters as Mudheads, Longhorns and six Shalako, always men. The ceremony starts at dusk when the six Shalako dancers gather outside the south side of the Zuni Pueblo village. The Shalako figure, twice the size of a tall man, is awesome. The costume worn by this figure has a mask with protruding pop-eyes, a long beaked nose, horns, and a gigantic, all-feather neck ruff. The bottom half of the costume is made of Hopi Indian blankets wrapped around a body of wooden undersupports.

The ceremonial calls for the Shalako to cross the south bridge (with their attendants) into the village where they doff the full "body mask" costumes. They eat in previously-selected houses that have been newly repaired or built, and usually there are eight host houses. The Shalako return in the night, while a chorus chants continuously. They pray for several hours, feast on local foods, and finally perform hypnotic dances to music from pottery drums. By dawn the ceremonial is over, and the six Shalako return over the south bridge of the community. Ritual races follow.

To attend Shalako is to step out of ordinary life into another realm of experience. It is a ceremony that ends a 49-day period when the Zunis build new housing. The flooring is not placed in a new house until after the Shalako ceremony because the deities need to be in touch with the earth when they dance.

The Zunis are rightly famous for their handwork. They are masters who inlay jewelry with turquoise, jet, shell and silver. Their carved fetishes in many animal forms are collector's items. They do "needlepoint" in silver. And, they make charming beaded dolls from a few inches to two feet tall, in addition to kachinas.

It is well worth the time to visit the restored mission church of Our Lady of Guadalupe. There are tours starting from the St. Anthony rectory (782-4477). The walls are painted with images from the Zuni religion done by Alex Seowtewa. The left wall represents the spring and summer ceremonies and the right wall the autumn and winter ones. A mosaic of the Virgin Mary of Guadalupe hangs above the altar. The building is a tribute to the ecumenical spirit that binds the Zuni people.

Over Labor Day weekend there is also an annual fair and rodeo at Zuni.

USEFUL ADDRESSES

Eight Northern Indian Pueblo Council
P.O. Box 969
San Juan Pueblo, New Mexico 87566
505/852-4265

The Council not only helps its member pueblos in their ventures, but also sponsors the annual crafts show in mid-July. (The show is currently held at San Ildefonso.)

Indian Pueblo Cultural Center
2401 12th St. NW
Albuquerque, New Mexico 87102
505/843-7270

The Center has a museum, a gallery for arts and crafts, and a restaurant, and sponsors tours to various pueblo dances and events.

Inter-Tribal Indian Ceremonial
P.O. Box 1
Church Rock, New Mexico 87311
505/863-3896

This group sponsors the annual intertribal event that takes place in Gallup every year in mid-August.

New Mexico Hotel and Motel Association
P.O. Box 5713
Santa Fe, New Mexico 87502-5713
505/982-9771

The Association will send an up-to-date directory of lodgings on request.

Southwestern Association on Indian Affairs
P.O. Box 1964
Santa Fe, New Mexico 87504-1964
505/983-5220

This organization is dedicated to preserving Indian cultural heritage, and it sponsors the world-famous annual Indian Market held in Santa Fe in mid-August.

State of New Mexico
Economic Development and Tourism Department
Joseph M. Montoya Building
1100 St. Francis Drive
Santa Fe, New Mexico 87503
(505) 827-0291

This office will send visitors a packet of materials including an annual vacation guide and maps.

CALENDAR OF INDIAN DOINGS

Almost all dates are variable.
See pueblo listings for individual phone numbers and call in advance.

January

1	Most pueblos, including Taos, Santo Domingo, San Felipe, Cochiti, Santa Ana, Picuris	*Turtle, Corn and various other dances*
6	Most northern and southern pueblos	*Kings' Day; installation of new governors and officials. Animal dances*
23	San Ildefonso	*Annual feast day in honor of St. Ildefonse. Comanche, Animal dances*
25	Picuris	*Various dances*
27	San Juan	*Basket dance*

February

First week	Acoma	*Governor's Feast; various dances*
2	San Felipe and other pueblos	*Candelaria Day; various dances*
4-5	Taos	*Los Comanches dance*
Var.	San Juan	*Deer dance*
Var.	Santa Clara	*Animal dances*
Var.	Isleta	*Evergreen dance*

March

19	Old Laguna Village	*Annual feast day in honor of St. Joseph. Harvest and social dances*
Easter	Most pueblos	*Various dances*

May

1	San Felipe	*Annual feast day in honor of St. Joseph. Harvest and social dances*
3	Cochiti, Taos	*Santa Cruz Day; coming of the Rivermen. Green Corn dance, traditional foot races*
Var.	Tesuque	*Blessing of the fields. Corn or Flag dance*

June

13	Sandia	*Annual feast day in honor of St. Anthony. Corn dance*
	Cochiti	*Grab Day*
	San Ildefonso, San Juan, Santa Clara, Taos, Picuris or various other dances	*Annual feast day in honor of St. Anthony. Corn, Comanche*
23-24	San Juan	*Annual feast day in honor of St. John the Baptist. Buffalo dance, evening of 23rd; War dances, foot races on 24th*
24	Taos	*Annual feast day in honor of St. John the Baptist. Corn dance*
	Cochiti	*Annual feast day in honor of St. John the Baptist. Grab day*
29	Acoma	*Annual feast day in honor of St. Peter. Rooster pull*
	San Felipe, Santa Ana Santo Domingo	*Annual feast day in honor of St. Peter. Corn dance*

July

1-4	Mescalero	*Mescalero Apache Gahan Ceremonial*
4	Nambe	*Nambe Falls Ceremonial; various dances*
14	Cochiti	*Annual feast day in honor of St. Bonaventure. Corn dance*

Var.	San Ildefonso	*Annual Eight Northern Pueblos Arts & Crafts Show*
20	San Juan	*Annual Popé foot race*
25	San Ildefonso, Taos	*Annual feast day in honor of St. James; various dances*
	Acoma, Cochiti, San Felipe Laguna, Santo Domingo	*Annual feast day in honor of St. James. Grab day*
26	Santa Ana	*Annual feast day in honor of St. Ann. Corn dance*
Last Weekend		
	Santa Clara	*Puye Cliffs Ceremonial. Various dances*

August

2	Jemez	*Old Pecos Bull and Corn dances*
4	Santo Domingo	*Annual feast day in honor of St. Dominic. Corn dance*
5-10	All pueblos	*Symbolic relay run*
9-10	Picuris	*Annual feast day in honor of St. Lawrence. Sunset dance, evening of 9th; dances, foot races on 10th*
10	Acomita village, Acoma	*Annual feast day in honor of St. Lawrence. Corn dance*
	Laguna, Cochiti	*Annual feast day in honor of St. Lawrence. Grab Day*
12	Santa Clara	*Annual feast day in honor of St. Clare. Harvest, Comanche or Buffalo dances*
Mid-August		
	Gallup	*Intertribal ceremonial*
15	Zia	*Feast of the Assumption. Corn dance*
	Mesita village, Laguna	*Annual feast day in honor of St. Anthony. Harvest and social dances*
28	Isleta	*Spanish and Indian fiestas*

September

2	Acoma	*Annual feast day in honor of St. Stephen. Harvest dances*
4	Isleta	*Annual feast day in honor of St. Augustine. Harvest dance*
8	Encinal village, Laguna	*Feast of the Nativity. Harvest and social dances.*
	San Ildefonso	*Corn dance*
14-15	Stone Lake, Dulce	*Jicarilla Apache Fair. Rodeos, pow-wows, foot races, dances*
Var.	Window Rock, Arizona	*Window Rock Navajo Fair*
19	Old Laguna	*Annual feast day in honor of St. Joseph. Harvest dance*
25	Paguate village, Laguna	*Annual feast day in honor of St. Elizabeth. Harvest and social dances*
29-30	Taos	*Annual feast day in honor of St. Jerome. Sundown dance, evening of 29th. War and various dances, trade fair, races and pole climbing on 30th*
Last week	San Juan	*Harvest dance*

October

First week	Shiprock	*Annual Navajo Fair*
4	Nambe	*Annual feast day in honor of St. Francis. Various dances*
17	Paraje Village, Laguna	*Annual feast day in honor of St. Margaret Mary. Harvest and social dances*

November

12	Jemez	*Annual feast day in honor of San Diego. Corn dance*
	Tesuque	*Annual feast day in honor of San Diego. Flag, Buffalo, Deer or Comanche dance*

December

Var.	Zuni	*Shalako Ceremonial. Blessing of new homes*
Var.	Navajo (Window Rock)	*Navajo Nightway and Mountaintop Way ceremonies*
12	Jemez	*Annual feast day in honor of Our Lady of Guadalupe. Matachines Dance*
	Pojoaque	*Annual feast day in honor of Our Lady of Guadalupe. Comanche, Buffalo, Bow and Arrow or Butterfly dance*
24-25	San Juan	*Matachines dance, religious procession*
	Taos	*Sundown torchlight procession of the Virgin after vespers on 24th. Deer or Matachines dance on 25th*
	Picuris	*Matachines dances*
25	San Ildefonso, Santa Clara	*Matachines dances*
	Tesuque	*Matachines or deer dance*
	Jemez, Santa Ana, San Felipe, Santo Domingo, Cochiti	*Animal, Harvest, Basket, Rainbow, Matachines and various other dances*
26	San Juan	*Turtle dance*
28	Santa Clara	*Holy Innocence Day. Various children's dances*

Studying the past at the School of American Research in Santa Fe.

NORTHERN NEW MEXICO GLOSSARY

ADOBE: One of the oldest building materials known to man, the bricks of clay-bearing soil, straw and water have been used for centuries in Santa Fe as insulators against cold winters and summer heat. Adobe is a popular, relatively inexpensive building material around the world. Once the soil, straw, and water are mixed, the bricks are baked in the sun to a rugged consistency before use. Many older Santa Fe dwellings and structures are built entirely of adobe.

ANASAZI CULTURE: The most influential and progressive culture to spring up in the Southwest's intriguing past, the Anasazi ("the ancient ones") first emerged in the region around the time of the death of Christ. Although not the oldest culture in the Southwest, the Anasazi proved themselves masters of their time during a 500-year "golden age" around 1000 A.D. Traces of their unique talents still baffle historians and archaeologists ill-prepared to explain the highly advanced culture known for outstanding architectural and masonry innovations, weaving and pottery with intricate geometric designs. The Anasazi, as master builders, constructed massive houses of stone and mud plaster with common walls. Remains of large subterranean ceremonial chambers used as the civilization's sacred kivas were uncovered long after the reign of the Ancient Ones was over. The Anasazi culture disappeared as mysteriously as it had began. Whether the end of the Anasazi presence resulted from pestilence and disease or drought has never been established.

ARROYO: Nature's drainage and flood control system throughout the arid New Mexico deserts. Arroyos are to be avoided by rock hounds, particularly during the summer rainy season when the dry gullies can turn into raging rivers within minutes. Arroyos are also favored dens for snakes and other reptiles.

BARRIO DE ANALCO: Analco, an Aztec Indian word meaning "the other side of the water," marked the segregation line of the homes of Tlaxcala Indian servants from the Spanish who lived near what is now the Plaza in downtown Santa Fe. The Tlaxcala Indian servants were brought to Santa Fe by the Spanish in the 1600s. The neighborhood, across the river from the Inn at Loretto, today is one of the oldest settlements in the nation.

BURRO ALLEY: Burro pack trains and caravans hauling commodities and wood used this alley in downtown Santa Fe as the main entrance to the village for commerce and barter for more than a century. The present Palace Restaurant courtyard sits where a stable area was until the 1940s; a cache of gold jewelry was unearthed in the stable area in the 1920s.

CÁBEZA DE VACA, ALVAR NÚÑEZ: This seafaring explorer, shipwrecked off the Texas coast in 1528, may well have been the original purveyor of the tales of the Seven Cities of Cibola (seven cities of gold). He and other survivors of the sea disaster roamed the Southwest for eight years before arriving in Mexico City, telling the story of villages in the north where gold was as plentiful as sand. The tale of untold wealth in the reputed Seven Cities of Cibola prompted the later expedition by Francisco Vásquez de Coronado. The Seven Cities of Cibola were never found.

CAMINO REAL: Wagon ruts still remain today in many isolated areas of New Mexico on this famous trail blazed by the Spaniards as the Royal Highway from Mexico City reaching through Santa Fe. The road generally follows Agua Fria Street through the City Different; historical groups are seeking national landmark status for the road.

CERRILLOS: Some of the world's finest turquoise was mined from the "little hills" and mountains of this area south of Santa Fe on Hwy. 14 (the Turquoise Trail), home of the nation's oldest designated mining district. Cerrillos turquoise was unique in its quality; revered by Pueblo Indians in religious ceremonies who called it "the sky in the stone." Spanish, Indians and, eventually, rugged pioneers came in search of the gemstones. The Tiffany turquoise mine turned out millions of dollars of the gemstones. The mine is sometimes open to tours. Turquoise tailings litter the surface outside. Silver, gold, lead, and zinc were also extracted from the mountains pushed up by volcanic eruptions in pre-historic times. Cerrillos was a boom town in the 1800s and supported 21 saloons for the hard-working, hard-drinking miners. Movie studios discovered the Old West ambiance of Cerrillos in recent years; *Young Guns*, about New Mexico's best known desperado, Billy The Kid, was filmed at Cerrillos.

CHILE: Red or green? A staple in the cuisine of New Mexicans for centuries. Red chile, ripened longer on the vine, is the smoother, while green chile is somewhat hotter. Both are rich in vitamin C. Chile has been prescribed in herbal folklore for everything from nursing a hangover to fighting a cold.

CHIMAYÓ: Three centuries ago, convicts were exiled or banished to this mountain community by the Spanish. Santuario de Chimayó, a penitent chapel built in 1817, is the most noted landmark and the only miraculous shrine in the United States. Every year on Good Friday, thousands of pilgrims trek to the shrine for healings from the alleged curative power of the earth from a well near the alter. Since the early 1700s, Chimayó has been a major Spanish weaving center. A fortified plaza, Plaza de Cerro, also graces the village.

CORONADO, FRANCISCO VÁSQUEZ DE: He roamed the Southwest from 1540-1542 with 1,000 soldiers from Mexico under his command in an exasperating and futile search for the fabled Seven Cities of Cibola. Coronado returned home in disgrace when his expedition failed to find the fabled wealth, but he saw and visited permanent Indian dwellings in the Southwest. He named them *pueblos*, Spanish for towns.

COYOTE: The wily critter, often the trickster in Indian folk tales, is on its way to becoming Santa Fe's unofficial mascot. Small and large wooden replicas of the wolf-like animal are for sale throughout Santa Fe. The coyote has been part of Southwestern folklore for centuries.

CRISTO REY CHURCH: Built of more than 180,000 adobe bricks, Cristo Rey Church, located off Canyon Road in Santa Fe, is one of the best examples of New Mexico Spanish mission architecture and one of the largest modern adobe structures in the nation. The church houses the carved stone *reredo* (altar screen) commissioned by Governor Francisco Antonio Marin del Valle completed in 1760-61. The reredo is recognized in the National Register of Historic Places. The church was dedicated in 1940 to commemorate the 400th anniversary of Coronado's arrival in the upper Rio Grande Valley.

CROSS OF THE MARTYRS: From a hilltop providing a panoramic view of Santa Fe, this memorial recalls nearly 1,500 years of Santa Fe history and honors the 23 Franciscan priests killed in the 1680 Pueblo Revolt. A walkway park, opened in 1986, includes 20 plaques denoting Santa Fe's unique past. The original Cross of the Martyrs is on a hill to the west of Majors Field. The two crosses can be seen from each other.

DE VARGAS, DON DIEGO: De Vargas, celebrated as a local hero especially during Fiesta, was chosen by the Viceroy of New Spain to reconquer Santa Fe in 1692 after the 1680 Pueblo Revolt drove the Spanish from New Mexico. He encountered heavy resistance from Indian warriors, but retook the Palace of the Governors in a fierce battle. He ordered 70 defenders executed and enslaved hundreds of others. Upon his own death later, de Vargas was thought to have been buried beneath one of the towers once standing at the corners of the Palace of the Governors or at a site which is now beneath the intersection of Palace Avenue and Washington Street.

FAROLITO: This Santa Fe-style Christmas decoration is used to illuminate and outline homes and buildings with soft light from candles anchored in sand-filled brown paper bags. Santa Feans each year trek throughout the city, particularly along Canyon Road and at the downtown Plaza, to view the spectacular on Christmas Eve.

FORT MARCY: The first U.S. Army fort in the Southwest was built in 1846 when U.S. troops laid claim to Santa Fe. The structure had walls nine feet high and five feet thick, encircled by an eight-foot-deep moat. The military settled in the Palace of the Governors and Plaza area and the fort was never occupied. Little remains of the fort other than small mounds of adobe and faint signs where the moat was excavated.

GLORIETA: On March 28, 1862, this one-time rest stop and watering hole east of Santa Fe became the site of a bloody battle between Union troops from Colorado and Confederate forces from Texas during the Civil War. The Confederate forces had captured Santa Fe only two weeks earlier, but were overwhelmed at Glorieta by the Union troops. The tranquil setting at Glorieta today includes a beautiful retreat built by the Southern Baptist Assembly.

JÉMEZ MOUNTAINS: Among the most majestic in north-central New Mexico, the Jémez Mountains begin their rise north of Albuquerque near the town of Bernalillo, first to about 5,000 feet along Santa Fe's distant western edges, then soaring to 11,000 feet west of Los Alamos. The mountain range was born more than 540 million years ago. Volcanic materials millions of years old top the range today. Jémez canyons abound with fossils and archaeology; climatic extremes of the range include all of the life zones of North America.

KIVA: Pueblo men constructed this sacred shelter for ceremonial rites, social or political gatherings. The underground shelter was usually entered by a smoke hole in the roof. Religious treasures were also stored in the kiva. The Santa Fe-style kiva fireplace is modeled after the fire pit and ventilator shaft used in the sacred shelters.

LAMY, JEAN BAPTISTE: This prominent religious figure was elevated to Santa Fe's first archbishop by the Pope on Feb. 12, 1875. Born Oct. 11, 1814, in Lempdes, Puy-de-Dom France, Lamy was the driving force behind construction of Saint Francis Cathedral and brought the Christian Brothers and Sisters of Loretto to Santa Fe. Lamy, who died Feb. 14, 1888, and is buried in the cathedral, was remembered in "Death Comes to The Archbishop," by Willa Cather.

LORETTO CHAPEL: This was the first Gothic building west of the Mississippi completed in 1878 modeled after the Sainte Chapelle in Paris, but its most renowned claim to fame is the Miraculous Staircase. The Sisters of Loretto, brought to Santa Fe in 1857 by Archbishop Lamy, were exasperated to notice that builders had forgotten to erect a passageway from the ground floor to the choir loft. They prayed to St. Joseph, patron saint of carpenters, for guidance. Not long thereafter, an elderly man riding a donkey arrived and offered his help. Using only a saw, t-square and hammer, he built a 33-step staircase with two 360-degree turns with wooden pegs instead of nails. There were no center or side supports, defying all known engineering principles at the time. When the job was completed, the old man vanished as mysteriously as he had arrived. The Sisters of Loretto considered the miracle Divine Intervention; some townspeople said the wood used in the stairway was not native to New Mexico and they could find no records where the old man may have purchased the timber. The stairway continued in daily use until 1968, but still remains today as a miracle of engineering.

LOWRIDERS: Common to northern New Mexico, lowriders are customized vintage classics such as Ford LTDs, Chevy Impalas, or Buick Rivieras modified with plush interiors and hydraulic suspension systems to raise and lower and the fronts and backs of the cars. They are favored by Hispanic car clubs for cruising the Santa Fe Plaza on warm summer evenings. Movie producer and actor Robert Redford arrived on the Plaza in a lowrider rather than a limo for the premiere of *The Milagro Beanfield War.*

LUMINARIA: On Christmas Eve in Santa Fe, fragrant piñon logs are stacked and burned along winding, quaint streets, symbolically lighting the way for shepherds to find the Christ child born that night in a humble Bethlehem stable when there was no room in the inn.

MADRID: This coal mining town south of Santa Fe has been revived by artists, craftsmen and entrepreneurs to step back to the late 1800s when Madrid was a booming village of 3,000. Madrid became a ghost town in the 1950s when the demand for coal declined; weathered frame cabins dot the landscape. Visitors may tour vintage mining equipment or go into one of the mines to see a coal seam. Numerous souvenir shops abound; live entertainment is available in an old saloon; quaint restaurants offer local cuisine.

NAMBÉ: The name is more commonly associated today with unusual decorative cookware manufactured since 1951, but Nambé is also one of the pueblos north of Santa Fe. Nambé ware, however, has gained international fame. A manufacturing plant operates in Santa Fe.

OLDEST HOUSE: Common of the dwellings in the Barrio de Analco across Old Santa Fe Trail, the original foundations of this house allegedly were laid by the Pueblo Indians in the 13th century. Folklore has it that the first white occupant was a Franciscan padre accompanying Coronado in 1541. Historians argue whether, in fact, it is the oldest house. Available maps do not show a structure at that location until around 1770. The house, however, is an excellent example of old adobe construction; the walls are of "puddled adobe" rather than conventional bricks. Windows face away from the mountains as Indians saved these views for special occasions.

PALACE OF THE GOVERNORS: The oldest public building in continuous use in the nation, the Palace of the Governors was built in 1610-1612 when La Villa de Santa Fe was founded. The Palace (*El Palacio Real*) has been the seat of six governments under different flags. Indians captured it from the Spanish in the 1680 Pueblo Revolt when it was used as a fortress. Governor Lew Wallace lived there in the 1880s. Wallace was better known as the scriptwriter of *Ben Hur*. The Legislature appropriated funds in 1909 to convert the building into the Museum of New Mexico to house the historical division of the state museum system.

PAWN JEWELRY: Native Americans often used prized personal jewelry to trade for other commodities. Little of genuine trade jewelry remains on the market today. Pawn-style jewelry, however, is abundant in local shops. Items declared as genuine pawn jewelry should be authenticated.

PECOS: Named after a local tribe as a surviving pueblo, this step back into history offers an inspiring lesson with the ruins of an ancient pueblo and a magnificent mission. Hiking, camping, and horseback riding are favorite pastimes in the region. The pueblo was briefly abandoned in 1838 when only 17 villagers remained.

PERALTA, DON PEDRO DE: Founder of La Villa de Santa Fe, he was the city's first Spanish governor. De Peralta relocated the capital at Santa Fe as a more central location on orders from King Ferdinand and Queen Isabella. The capital had earlier been at San Juan Bautista.

POT HUNTING: Many visitors to New Mexico find themselves intrigued with the prospects of finding artifacts to take home as souvenirs. The state has 50,000 known archaeological sites recording more than 10,000 years of human history. Anything form arrowheads to calvary remnants can turn up; however, because artifacts hold still more secrets to the state's heritage, stealing or defacing artifacts on state or federal lands is a criminal offense punishable by fines up to $100,000 and/or five years in prison.

PUBLIC TRANSPORTATION: The Chile Line tour bus system is the only means of public transportation in Santa Fe. Taxi service is available, but most visitors choose private vehicles. The Pride of Taos Shuttle fills the transportation gap in Taos.

PUEBLO REVOLT: Popé of San Juan Pueblo led a successful uprising against the Spanish to drive them from the Palace of the Governors in August 1680 after 80 years of persecution by the *conquistadores*. During the battle, 23

Franciscan priests and friars were killed by the incensed Indians. The Spanish retreated to what is now El Paso, Texas. The Spanish recaptured Santa Fe 12 years later, led by Don Diego de Vargas.

PUYE CLIFF DWELLINGS: The Puye dwellings in the Pajarito Plateau region of northern New Mexico were initially caves hollowed into cliffs and where pueblos were later built along the slopes above the mesa. For three centuries, Pueblo Indians inhabited the dwellings. Eventually, two levels of the cliff dwellings were joined with the 740-room pueblo by ladders. A great community house, ceremonial chamber and petroglyphs still remain. The dwellings apparently were abandoned about 1580 when drought and failed crops forced the inhabitants to move elsewhere. The dwellings today are owned by Santa Clara Pueblo. The cliffs have been designated as a National Historic Landmark.

RISTRA: A bundle of red chiles usually found hanging in the sun for drying. In northern New Mexico, ristras can be found hanging today more as decoration than the local method of drying the chiles for recipes. Ristras are for sale throughout northern New Mexico. Onions or garlic are also hung in bunches for drying.

SAINT FRANCIS CATHEDRAL: Completed in 1886, the cathedral is the most photographed structure in Santa Fe. Located downtown at the top of San Francisco Street, the cathedral is also the home for *La Conquistadora* (Our Lady of the Conquest), the oldest Marian image in the U.S., arriving in 1625. The cathedral is located on the site of the first parish church built in 1610. Masses are said daily.

SANGRE DE CRISTO MOUNTAINS: Spanish for "Blood of Christ Mountains." Sunsets reflecting off the mountains east of Santa Fe often leave the peaks aglow in crimson; hence the name. Legend has it that when the 1680 Pueblo Revolt began, a frightened padre asked for a sign from God while Franciscan priests were being killed. The padre saw the snowcapped peaks of the mountains bathed in shades of crimson. The legend has survived three centuries.

SAN MIGUEL MISSION: Although not the oldest church in New Mexico, San Miguel Mission is the oldest church in continuous use in the United States. The first church at this site was built in 1626 for the Tlaxcalan Indian servants, but was destroyed in the 1680 Pueblo Revolt. The present chapel was built in 1710 and has been maintained by the Christian Brothers since 1859. It houses a wooden *reredo* (altar screen) built in 1798, many artifacts and examples of 18th century religious art. The San Jose Bell, whose history is still debated by historians, is in the gift shop. The Christian Brothers claim it was cast in 1356 in Andalucia and rang in Spain and Mexico for 450 years before being brought to Santa Fe in 1812. The Historic Santa Fe Foundation, however, claims it was molded by an itinerant bellcaster in 1856 who simply wasn't the best. The Foundation claims the sandcasting was defective and only makes the date appear to be 1356.

SANTA FE PLAZA: For more than three centuries, the Plaza has been the soul of Santa Fe's social, economic and political life. The Viceroy under King Ferdinand III decreed in 1610 that the Plaza be modeled to resemble Santa Fe, Granada, today the City Different's sister city. The Pueblo Revolt against the Palace of the Governors was launched from the Plaza in 1680 by Indian leader Popé. The Plaza became a historic landmark in 1962.

SANTA FE RAILWAY: The famous rail line was built to follow the Santa Fe Trail, but the line never came to Santa Fe because the city wasn't willing to pay for the train service. Only a freight spur was completed into town. Even today, rail passengers must travel to Lamy, south of Santa Fe, to board Amtrak.

SANTUARIO DE NUESTRA SEÑORA DE GUADALUPE: The santuario is the oldest surviving church in the U.S. dedicated to the Virgin of Guadalupe, the most revered saint in Latin America. Built nearly 200 years ago, the santuario was refurbished in 1975 after being abandoned for 14 years. It was once an authentic example of an 18th century New Mexico church, but fell to the ravages of fire, the elements, and neglect. Today it has the flavor of a California mission and is home to the Santa Fe Desert Chorale. A canvas of the Virgin of Guadalupe painted in Mexico in 1783 hangs in the altar area.

SENA PLAZA: Don Juan Sena bought this tract of land in what is now downtown Santa Fe in 1796 to build a home for his wife. His heir, Jose Desiderio Sena, built it into a 33-room hacienda in the 1800s for his 23 children. When the territorial capitol burned in 1892, the Legislature met in the second story ballroom. The scenic plaza today houses unique shops and restaurants.

STORYTELLER: Figurines, usually black, white or brown, of an Indian woman seated with small children on her lap.

TURQUOISE: The official state gem, the semiprecious stone had sacred and spiritual significance to Southwest Indian tribes over the centuries. A blue or blue-green mineral of aluminum and copper, the turquoise lodes were formed by volcanic activity, then thousands of years of compression and leaching. The Pueblo Indians call the gem "the sky in the stone." Legend has it that those who wear turquoise ward off misfortune and disease.

VALLE GRANDE: In the Chama region near Los Alamos, Valle Grande is the site of the largest extinct volcano caldera in the world. When the summit of the million-year-old volcano collapsed, a pastoral, lush mountain valley 18 miles long and 12 miles across was formed. Lava domes, however, block the view across the entire basin. Valle Grande is also called the Valle Caldera and the Great Jemez Crater.

ZOZOBRA: One of the newest traditions in Santa Fe, it was the brainchild of Santa Feans Will Shuster and Jacques Cartier in 1926 to release personal anxieties during Fiesta. The notion was to build a paper mache monster representing depression, gloom and uncertainty and burn the 40-foot monster, symbolically destroying fears of misfortunes, past and present. Tens of thousands attend the ritual burning of Old Man Gloom at Fort Marcy Park during Fiesta celebrations each September. Zozobra, although not an age-old tradition, has become a symbol of Santa Fe's magical and mystical history.